Praise for

CAREGIVING FOR ELDERLY PARENTS

Marky and Dauna share their personal stories as daughters of aging and dying parents. Through alternating and very different voices, they offer their insights into their new roles as adult caregivers. These pages are filled with bittersweet moments, humor, practical advice, and many tearful and joyful memories - all cradled in grace and love. For those of us facing both the physical and mental decline of our elder loved ones, Marky and Dauna teach us and assure us we are not alone. Adding additional personal touches are Gary's charming watercolor illustrations and the photos of these two loving multigenerational families.

Carol Hogan, MLS
School Librarian
Issaquah, Washington

Marky and Dauna's message focuses on the blessings of taking care of parents: the hard-won, heart-felt blessings of honoring one's parents with care and compassion at a time in their life when they can't necessarily respond in kind. Marky and Dauna touch on the forgiveness of old wounds—the kind that families unintentionally inflict on each other as parents raise children without any sort of manual—by children who suddenly find themselves in the midst of making life-changing decisions for parents who were their benchmarks, who held expectations for them, and against whom they measured success for much of their life. There are wonderful tidbits and practical how-to's mixed with self-deprecating humor and honesty so it reads as a guidebook for the mind and soul and encouragement for those who face similar experiences. Through laughter, lists, arguments, trial-and-error, guessing, grief, and grace you see how Marky and Dauna become the stabilizing bread in their club-sandwich family, as they reluctantly but necessarily take over the roles of matriarchs from their mothers and reframe their life.

I admit that I am not there yet in my familial relationships as my parents are just sighting 70. Thankfully, they are healthy of body and sound of mind still volunteering in their community and working the land, which allows me to live in a different state in contented pursuit of my own path. However, reading the vignettes has provided insight to my mother's selflessness as I watched her throughout her married life take care of her parents, in-laws, and aunts and uncles whose children were absent. I count myself lucky to be have been raised by such a woman who embodies the kindness, fortitude, integrity, and spirit that Marky and Dauna have. I think all of us worry: are we up to the task? How will we manage? Do I have the patience? Will I still be able to hear their love and laughter through any mental haze or physical infirmities? Will I know them? Will they still be my parents, even if I am making the decisions? And if yes, then what does that make me, exactly?

Truly, I hope that when it is my turn I can honor my parents in the same way these ladies have and count my blessings, even when I am feeling more like wilted lettuce than fresh bread.

Lisa Hechtman, Principal
Skyline High School
Issaquah School District

Most people don't want to read really long book reviews, so I will restrain myself. But if this were just about writing, I could write about this book most of the day. I have read countless books about aging, caregiving, and other "senior" issues, but this one is my favorite. Alternatively poignant and funny, and completely personal, **Caregiving Elderly Parents** *allows the reader to feel more like a family member. The authors, Marky Olson and Dauna Easley, welcome you into generations of their families to tell the stories of what they actually went through with both of their parents. Unlike books written purely for information, this one surrounds the information with a cocoon of humor and hard-won wisdom that feels real.*

Reading it, I got the "I can't wait to find out what's next" feeling of a good novel. While the title suggests that this book is for adult children who are aware that caregiving could be in their future, I think that just as much value could be realized by the parents themselves, the seniors who might soon need care. In fact, I want to admonish you, if you are getting on in years and don't want to be one of those difficult parents who won't accept aging, to read this book and put yourselves in the place of the authors. I can guarantee you, if you do, your elder years will be sweeter and more fulfilling for you and your children.

Steve Bogen, CFP®
Vice-President, Care-Finders Inc. and Insurance Recovery

For those of us in the baby boom era with elderly parents who have health issues, **Caregiving Elderly Parents** *by Marky Olson and Dauna Easley is the "Go To" book for both practical and heart felt advice. The scope of the book is broad, ranging from useful guidelines for how to choose the right skilled nursing facility to how to* write a proper medical directive. Equal attention is given to the emotional issues, such as how to truly listen to your parents so their dignity and respect are preserved. The authors are engaging as they tell their deeply personal stories. **Caregiving Elderly Parents** will make you both cry and laugh. Most of all, the sheer honesty of the writing is captivating. You'll be simultaneously entertained and educated."

Janis Heaphy
Retired Publisher and President
Sacramento Bee
Sacramento, California

A true end of life story. As one moves closer to the end of life, the guidance and insight that Marky and Dauna share shed honest light into what it means to care for a loved one. They bring heart filled love, paired with the ability to navigate the medical, ethical and family situations that we all must face. Their experience and wisdom is the gift this book offers.

Rev. Jana Smith-Worden, BCC
Hospice Chaplain
Good Samaritan Hospital
Tacoma, Washington

CAREGIVING
for Your
ELDERLY PARENTS

Real Stories to Help You Care for Your Loved Ones

Sharing Tips and Encouragement for the Sandwich Generation

MARKY OLSON, M.ED.
& DAUNA EASLEY, M.ED.

Caregiving for Your Elderly Parents
Real Stories to Help You Care for Your Loved Ones

©2012 by Marky Olson and Dauna Easley
All Rights Reserved. No part of this book may be used or reproduced in any manner whatsoever without the expressed written permission of the author.

Address all inquiries to:
Marky Olson and Dauna Easley
www.CaregivingElderlyParents.com

ISBN: 978-1-938686-09-2

Library of Congress Control Number: 2012950063

Illustrations: Gary C. Mathews
Cover Design & Interior Layout: Fusion Creative Works, www.fusioncw.com

Special Acknowledgement
Illustrator Gary C. Mathews is Marky's brother, adding deeper meaning to the stories. The original cover and chapter art reflect fun, memories and challenges depicted in the book. He lives on San Juan Island, WA, where his art reflects nature and all things marine. www.gcmathews.com

For additional copies, visit: www.CaregivingElderlyParents.com

Dedication

FOR OUR PARENTS

*By caring for us
they taught us how to care for them*

BETTY AND CRAIG MATHEWS

GINNIE SOWDERS

Introduction

Caring for elderly parents and loved ones can be a daunting task. In fact, the stress of doing so is a challenge too many of us are facing. We feel alone, because we love our parents and we're honor-bound to care for them. You may have siblings or a caring spouse by your side, but being unprepared, overwhelmed and guilt-ridden may still be what you feel. We have both cared for our parents, Marky for 7 years and Dauna continues to do so. As a result, we decided to create a resource to help you navigate this very challenging time of life.

We wrote about caring for our parents because, while many adult children are struggling with caregiving issues, many others are unaware of what is yet to come. If you are already a caregiver, you may be overwhelmed with caring for your own loved one. The challenges include housing, medical concerns, finances, communicating with a difficult parent, loneliness, downsizing, socializing, fear of the future and personal feelings you don't want to talk about. You may live close to your parent or far away; either situation presents difficult tasks and constant tests. And beyond logistics, all caregivers of elderly parents and loved ones experience an emotional upheaval that has the power to rock your world.

Are you feeling alone as you experience this new reality of taking care of a loved one? Are financial concerns keeping you awake? Did your parents neglect to plan for the challenges of aging? Are medical concerns overwhelming? If one of your parents is gone, is the living parent becoming completely dependent upon you for his or her ability to cope? Are your siblings unwilling to help with care-or worse-sabotaging your ability to care for your parents? Are you caught between helping your own children and your elderly parents?

And finally…

Are you a victim of that stealth robber of well-being: guilt?

If you've answered yes to any of the above questions, then take a deep breath and know that this book will become a resource and guide to help you through this stage of your life.

You probably aren't trained to be a caregiver, but because you want to help your parents, you are a caregiver. You will learn different ways to communicate with your parents and to help keep the guilt at bay and your own life in balance. You will be introduced to different housing choices and ideas for aging-in-place. You will learn how we communicated with medical professionals and professional caregivers. You will learn to be pro-active about financial concerns. These stories are real and you will feel the honesty. They will make you laugh and cry, while they also encourage, inform and inspire you.

You will find suggestions for many housing, medical and legal challenges within the Chapter Tips sections throughout the book. *More importantly, these stories will help you with the emotional upheaval you may be facing. Caregiving is as old as time, and love for one's parents is deeply universal. However, guilt can be a silent stalker with the power to sabotage your well-being.* Reading these stories will remind you that you're not alone. Within these pages you will learn from our mistakes *and* share in some of our ah-ha moments. You will learn that research and planning greatly reduce the stress of re-active decisions. And you will learn that you do not need to succumb to the power of guilt. You may even find your way to acceptance. We did.

We began teaching together in the early 1970s. Our paths lead us to different parts of the country, Seattle and Cincinnati. But the annual Christmas card kept us in touch. We love writing, are both professional speakers and are published in *Chicken Soup for the Soul*.

Marky wrote *Carry On, Mister Boy* for *Chicken Soup for the Soul Celebrates Dogs* and *Cooper and the Bride* for *What I Learned from the Dog*.

Dauna wrote *Lessons from the Greatest Teacher of My Life* for *A Fourth Course of Chicken Soup for the Soul*. Dauna has also written two books about teaching:

TEACH... To Change Lives

Teachers Touch Eternity.

We both earned under-graduate and graduate degrees from Miami University, Oxford, Ohio.

Each of us taught in the elementary grades and then went on to teach high school. Long marriages, children and grandchildren are the center of life for both of us.

Our Christmas-card friendship has rebuilt itself on the strength of the past and the new challenges of walking the final path with elderly parents. Dauna's parents are both still living. Marky's mother died in 2010 and her father passed away just as this book went to press.

We wrote this book to serve you and to put your mind at ease as you learn new strategies and to help you gain the emotional strength needed to care for your parents…and for yourself. Caregiving may be as old as time but we can help you navigate new ways to prepare. We want to help you learn how to do this for people you love. Let us be your guide as you walk this important journey.

Contents

Chapter One: The Elephant in the Room — 13

Chapter Two: The Sandwich Generation — 31

Chapter Three: Seniors vs. Seniors — 43

Chapter Four: Elder Needs — 53

Chapter Five: Safety Issues — 65

Chapter Six: Pets — 77

Chapter Seven: Doctor Visits — 87

Chapter Eight: Advocacy — 103

Chapter Nine: Nursing Homes — 117

Chapter Ten: Caregivers — 133

Chapter Eleven: Close vs. Far — 145

Chapter Twelve: Our Dads — 155

Chapter Thirteen: Memories and Patriotism — 165

Chapter Fourteen: Acceptance — 176

Epilogue: Home Before Dark — 187

Chapter One

THE ELEPHANT IN THE ROOM

MY PARENTS THEN. THE TALK. MY PARENTS NOW.

Marky writes

When the time comes for the tables to turn and the adult child becomes the parent of parents, looking back at how one was raised is inevitable. My childhood journey could be described as idyllic. I grew up in a small town where we ran free for hours. My mother was at home and my father was an engineer at General Mills in Lodi, California. The economic picture was very poor by today's standards, but I didn't know that. My father built our first ski boat-a 14' wooden craft propelled by a used 25 horse power Evinrude motor. We all learned to slalom ski on the local lake behind that handmade boat, propelled by that small engine. I remember spending hours watching my dad build that boat in our garage. From my mother, I learned the lifelong power of a beloved hobby-she sewed. She would pour over Vogue Magazine, draw pictures and make the clothes. Somehow, my parents found the money to take us snow skiing in the winter. We wore our only wool coats. Mine was long and plaid. I was a skiing princess.

In the summer, we towed our boat behind an old car to Lake Shasta where we camped and skied for two weeks. There were many flat tires and 25 cent watermelons from road stands on the way home…searches under the seats produced quarters to buy them. I rode my bike to school. My parents were always in the yearly talent show, still dancing and singing in my picture gallery of memories. The pictures certainly aren't digital, but they are indelibly imprinted in my mind and on my heart. I was loved unconditionally and I knew it.

My husband and I recently returned to my childhood home for a short visit. I loved seeing my old home and the town, but it was the lake that really took me back. Re-visiting the scene of the pure happiness of youth and its dancing memories has a power like no other.

My family lived within a day's drive of my parents all of the years we raised our daughters. Familial love was the basis, but my parents saw us as equals and the relationship mellowed into one of comfort, trust and camaraderie. We spent holidays and vacations together and the special link extended to our daughters. They took summer trips to visit by themselves. My husband's bond with my dad grew from endless home improvement projects, golf, watching sports and playing cards. Gin rummy was the game of choice. We would hear a loud "Gin" followed by devilish laughter. My mother and the girls and I did girl stuff. After visits, we returned to our respective full and productive lives.

Then my mother had a stroke.

I was a high school teacher by this time, our girls were out of college and one was married. The good choices I had made through my life and the trusting relationship we had built with my parents were to be tested repeatedly during the following years. My mother's first stoke became the dividing line of my life. My mother as I had known her was gone. The daughter she had known became her mother.

My parents moved to a Life Care Community in Olympia, a two hour drive from us. I learned to leave promptly after my last class on Friday; otherwise, the Friday traffic would double the time. Then, Mom suffered another stroke that left her wheelchair-bound, which is completely different than "needing a wheelchair to get around". One learns quickly about lifts, catheters, occupational therapists, skin sores resulting from compromised circulation, sinks and counters that are too high or too low and, if one is lucky, accessible vans. Woven around those needs, one learns about Medicare, endless specialists, hospital realities, a Durable Power of Attorney, Wills and Medical Directives. I haven't encountered anyone who actually wants to learn about such things. But you do if you want to survive.

If you haven't had the talk with your parents, you do because it's no longer just an elephant in the room; the elephant is now sucking the air out of the room.

You talk. You plan. You fight. You cry. And at some point, you move to the top of the familial hierarchy. My parents' life affairs were pretty straight-forward: the long-ago-written Will had been lost, the attorney was deceased and there was no long-term care insurance. On the plus side, my dad had retired with an excellent pension, as well as health insurance and he was a veteran. He was in good shape financially, but the money was tied to him, not Mom and her care needs doubled their cost of living.

We saw an attorney and left with a Will, a Medical Directive, Durable Power of Attorney (DPOA) and advice to get my name on their checking account. My father gifted me what money the law allowed, and moved his assets to an annuity which was in my name. Without the trust we had built, none of this would have happened. Without the DPOA, my name on their checking account and asset organization, my life would have been a nightmare. It wasn't exactly a cakewalk, but I slept most nights during the next 7 years that my parents lived.

Those details are the logistics, which filled and spilled over into the spare moments in my own busy life. It is far more difficult to describe emotions. Often, out of necessity or fear, emotions were denied or tabled until later for assessment. But there were moments when pure love and gratefulness were expressed in quiet eyes. Even when those feelings were expressed with words, they weren't as powerful as the uncertainty of silence.

During the last 5 years of my mother's life, she didn't really suffer from dementia. It was more that her personality was flat. The beautiful ups and downs of her laughter and unconditional love lost their animation. Still there, just very quiet. My father exhibited anger as he wrestled with what he saw as "the unfairness" of it all. He gradually adjusted during the last five years of Mom's life, then he suffered a stroke a year after she died. He survived, but in a state of dementia. Dementia has the power to cause deep heartache for those who love the sufferer. But I will give this to dementia: while it robs a person of self, at least it cocoons its crime in unawareness.

My Parents Aren't Ozzie and Harriet

Dawna writes

No, they aren't Ozzie and Harriet and I can prove it. As I write this my parents are both eighty-eight years old and relatively healthy. But at age eighty-eight *all* health is relative. They live independently, not even in retirement communities, but not together. They divorced when I was already an adult.

As a child I watched 1950s style sitcoms like Father Knows Best and Leave it to Beaver and wondered why I was living at the wrong address. I would have fit perfectly into the TV show's Ozzie and Harriet's family. I couldn't play the guitar like their son Ricky, but I loved to sing and dance. At Ozzie and Harriet's house the parents were calm and reasonable. They solved family problems with discussions. I was perfectly suited for that environment. I wanted to behave, do well in school, and please everyone. Instead I lived in typhoon alley, more like one of today's reality TV shows...the kind of show I currently use the remote control to avoid.

Unfortunately kids aren't born with a remote control for their lives. What was the big issue? My dad had girlfriends...*lots* of them. There are professional golf players and basketball stars who would be impressed by his stats on this issue. History books now suggest to us that JFK was a womanizer. Who knows? But back then presidents had the media protecting their privacy. And my mother was no Jackie Kennedy. Jackie seemed stoic about her situation, if it was true. My mother was the gurgling opposite. Mom reacted to Dad's flings like a flame to a keg of dynamite. And we kids were right in the middle of the continuing explosions.

Fights aside, my folks also didn't parent like Ozzie and Harriet either. On Saturdays when we would go with mom to the grocery store, the meat store, the discount store, the dairy etc. (Mom was always looking for the cheapest way to buy things) my sister Judy and I were allowed to have ten cents each, *if we were good,* to purchase something at the dime store. I'm aging myself here...think dollar store. One time we saw a small toy pop-up toaster that cost 29 cents. We loved the way those toy pieces of bread popped up. We begged mom for it. She said, "No" because it was nine cents extra and she thought we would fight over it. We continued to beg and swore we would share, so she finally relented.

On the way home we had a dispute in the backseat over the toaster. Mom calmly reached over the seat, grabbed our cherished new toaster, rolled down the car window and threw it out. She didn't even slow down. We didn't cry. We wouldn't dare. The punishment wasn't even what stunned us into silence. Mom had just thrown 29 cents out the window! The world could end on a day like that.

Nope, it sure wasn't Ozzie and Harriet. Who could imagine Harriet in her shirt waist dress throwing that toy out of the car window?

However, parts of my childhood were perfect for me. When I was seven we moved from our shack on the side of a hill to a modest baby boomer type subdivision in suburbia. I thought I was in heaven. Kids were everywhere and I loved being outside. I was athletic and popular in the neighborhood. I stayed outdoors from the time my chores were done until the lightning bugs appeared. I thrived in that environment. School was also easy for me and by third grade I had decided to become a teacher. I felt both safe and successful at school. I have a dim, sad memory of crying quietly at the end of a school day because I had to go back home to a house where parents were fighting. But always I told no one.

By the time I was ten I already felt like I was the most mature person in my household. Looking back I still agree with that assessment. But to be fair I was only a kid chronologically. I always seemed to be thirty-five on the inside. I placed high standards for behavior and initiative on myself even at a very young age. I forced myself to stay calm and reasonable no matter what was flying through the air around me. I placed a lot of pressure on myself to bring the crazies at home under control. Maybe for all these reasons I've described, it was a little easier for my mom and me when It came time to think about switching my role from child to parent-advisor as she aged.

I won't be writing as much about my dad in this book. We *do* have a relationship, but so far he has not required my care as he is married to someone other than my mother and still working. He is a courier delivering items within a three state area, yes even at age eighty-eight! I will write one piece about him later. But first you have to get to know me better, or you won't believe a word of it.

My mom is a child of the depression era and that fact has significantly colored her life. She worries about money every day. This fear was heightened when her own mother died when mom was only seven and her father, who was an alcoholic, deserted the family at the same time. Mom was raised by an older sister who didn't really want her. Mom expects the worst from life and is in a constant state of worry. A huge part of my role, as she sees it, is to take her worry away. I would like to turn this issue over to the United Nations and just giggle as they struggle to solve one more world problem that has no solution.

I'm the middle child of my parents' union and a baby boomer. I already have five grandchildren of my own. I choose to be very active in their lives also. I'm the primary caregiver for my mother but she has chosen to live independently in her own home for as long as she can. I have made a choice to support that decision. My daughter, Jodi, is in her thirties with five children of her own, but she has been extremely helpful to my mother. For many years I taught school while my daughter was home raising young children. She would pick up her grandma and take her along on excursions. Her grandma could sit in the van with the kids while Jodi ran errands for her family and my mother. They grew extremely close during those years. Jodi can grocery shop for her grandma and now frequently does. She calls grandma every day and can get away with a short phone conversation because she always has a child interrupting her or a carpool to drive.

Recently I was driving my granddaughter, Kiley, home from gymnastics. In a very circuitous way she asked me to do something for her. I can't remember the exact details.

The conversation went something like this.

> *Kiley, I'm impressed you worded that request very diplomatically.*

She surprised me with her reply.

> *Well, of course, I didn't want you to hit me or anything.*

I couldn't believe what she had just said to me.

> *Kiley. Think really hard. When have I ever hit you?*

She was quiet for a minute while she thought.

> *Well, you've never hit me. But once when I was little and sitting in the van with Grandma Ginnie while my mom was in a store, I talked back to Grandma Ginnie (my mother) because I didn't think I would get in trouble. She reached over the seat and whacked me with her cane.*

Nope, it sure wasn't Ozzie and Harriet. But whether you grew up in a Happy Days environment like my friend Marky, or stepped out of a scene from *One Flew Over the Cuckoo's Nest*, we all eventually face the same realities when our parents begin to age. Because of the way they parented us, or maybe even *in spite of the way they parented us*, how we step up to the task when *they* begin to need *us* is a reflection of our own moral compass. *It defines who **we** are.* I'm going to try my best to get it right. But, I confess, this is a bigger challenge than I ever thought it would be.

BEYOND THE BIRDS AND THE BEES

Dawna writes

I think I was in fifth grade when they marched all the girls in the fifth grade classes to the auditorium to see 'the movie'. Boys stayed in the classroom and weren't invited to the auditorium. What the heck was this all about? I was clueless. In spite of the fact that I had a sixth grade sister who had taken the walk to the auditorium only the year before, I had no idea what was happening.

Even more astonishing, as we walked into the auditorium I could see kids' mothers sitting far away from us in the bleachers... *including my own mother*! This was completely unbelievable to me. It was the 1950s and my mom was one of only two working mothers that I knew. She simply *never* took time off work. She didn't attend PTA meetings or any school functions. What in the world could be happening? This was during the era when Americans feared the acts of the Communists and some people built bomb shelters in their basements. My twin friends Terry and Sherry had shown me their bomb shelter in their basement. Could the Communists be coming for just the girls?

Needless to say that movie caught me completely unprepared. As this new information unfolded on the screen, I was even more uncomfortable because I knew my mom was in the room. I just kept thinking

> *Why are they making up all this stupid stuff **and worse,** telling it to my mother?*

Given any chance, I would have run from the room. But it was just too embarrassing to even consider looking right or left, let alone moving out of my chair. When I arrived home I was greeted by another horrible surprise. Mom was still home from work and asked me what I thought of the movie. What was the answer I gave her?

> *That was the dumbest movie I have ever seen in my life!*

I ran to the bathroom, closed the door and locked it. I stayed in the bathroom until I was sure that she would never approach me again. Dad came home and I could hear mom fixing dinner. That was the end of my entire sex education. That is the knowledge I carried in my suitcase on my honeymoon. I'm sure there was a discussion in my high school health class, but I had been so traumatized in fifth grade I effectively zoned out that day. My body was in the room but I essentially willed myself blind and deaf for an hour.

Fast forward fifty years. My friend Marky and I were talking by phone across the country about the challenges, fears, and emotions of helping our elderly parents cope with their health issues.

Marky asked me a question using a serious tone.

> *When did you have 'the talk' with your parents?*

I paused for a moment. Immediately I got nervous. My brain flashed back to fifth grade. Was I supposed to have told my mom about sex? Is that what I did wrong? Reluctantly I asked her.

What talk?

I was scared to death of what she might say next.

You know. The talk when your parents finally realize and admit that they may not be immortal, when they are ready to talk about giving you power of attorney to make medical decisions when they no longer can…or talk about a living will, that kind of thing…

Instantly I was relieved.

Oh, **that** *talk.*

Maybe because the sex talk had gone so badly, this second talk was relatively painless for Mom and me. If life has a way of balancing itself out, then we had definitely earned an easy conversation. It started with a post card and Mom's walking group. Mom was in her early seventies at the time. She walked between three and five miles at the local mall every day before the mall opened. Most of her walking buddies were also seniors. While walking Mom talked to them about a postcard she had received in the mail offering a free seminar on legal issues seniors needed to address. Her friends told her it was a good idea. They shared horror stories about probate court with her.

She approached me with the post card. At first I was leery. I was afraid it was someone who wanted to try and get mom to invest money with them. And frankly, I didn't want to think about mom dying. But as I read the postcard and asked my fellow teachers, I decided we had a lot to learn and this might be a way to start. We went to the seminar saying to each other

We're just going to go and learn what we can. We're not buying anything.

It was an extremely well organized half day seminar. It explained to us all the documents Mom and I needed to face her possible future health needs. It discussed living will choices and the sad things that happen when an estate goes into probate. Mom and I left that day informed. We talked it over together. She very much wanted to go through with it, but didn't want to spend the money. Did I mention that Mom was a child of the depression era? I told her if it was important to her I would pay the costs. We saw an attorney together and found out what decisions we had to make. Mom was quite healthy and it felt a little odd talking about all this stuff. But I am forever grateful that we did.

About five years later when Mom went by ambulance to the hospital I had only a few days to find a nursing home for Mom's temporary rehabilitation. It helped that I had all the correct forms at my fingertips. I have a complete notebook, furnished by the attorney, of everything I have ever needed to admit Mom into the hospital, provide a doctor permission to operate, or help Mom make a decision (we have already discussed) that she may later be unable to verbalize.

There is a key word I must mention here: **trust.** Without trust on both sides this may be a kamikaze mission. My mother is still making sound decisions and I support those decisions, even when others pressure me not to do so. She trusted me enough to know that I would do that. She also still trusts me enough to know that when she makes a decision that is not in her best interest, I will intervene.

I am quite amazed at the number of people who will step forward and offer an opinion even when none is solicited. I've had an occasional neighbor ambush me at my car door and give me their opinions about where I should put my mother. Sometimes I need my Mom's reassurance. I take her for regular doctor and physical therapy visits. She wears a life alert button twenty-four hours a day. I want her to be safe and well. But recently I had to ask her again, just for my own benefit.

> *Mom, one morning, when neither Jodi nor I can reach you by phone, and I come to your house and find you have passed away, I will be horribly upset. But then hopefully later I will feel like I have honored your wishes for you to die at home. Am I right about that? Is this still what you <u>really</u> want?*

She replied without any hesitation.

> *Absolutely. That is what I <u>really</u> want.*

I just needed to hear her say it again. And I'm not certain we will be that fortunate. Who knows what the future holds? But I know that she trusts me enough to make the change call if it has to be made. Mom and I may not have handled the birds and bees talk too well, but we delivered a 'slam dunk' the second time we had to have the talk. I'm proud of us.

TIPS FOR THE ELEPHANT IN THE ROOM

Dawna says

1. I was so lucky that Mom initiated this one. If your parent ever brings it up, don't shrink from it. It is the moment to move forward.

2. Ask around. Look for a good seminar. My mom and I learned together. It wasn't one of us forcing the other into anything. When the lawyer talked about the government taking her money away in probate she became all ears.

3. Truth is I miss my mom being my mom. Every once in a while I get a small dose of it and I am thankful for that moment.

4. I have become officially 'the parent' but I try my best to listen and honor Mom's choices whenever possible. I honestly don't treat her like a kid. I find I don't have to force her. If I give her a little longer to consider her choices, she will come to the right decision.

5. Laugh *with* your parent, not at them. Recently my daughter and son-in-law were exchanging looks and a laugh at my lackluster computer skills. I didn't like it and called them on it. I reminded them of the skills I have that they don't possess. They were instantly contrite. It helped me understand how my mom feels. Try to remember to walk in your parents' shoes. Changing

roles isn't always easy. Don't escalate the discomfort by laughing "at" them.

Marky says

1. <u>Talk</u>. Be willing to talk about death. No one wants to have this conversation, but it is essential. Find out how your parent feels about life-sustaining measures. Find out if they want to be cremated, have a traditional funeral, where they want to be buried. The first time I brought up the subject of death with my parents, they both said,

Oh, we never think about that.

Not such a great start. I pieced the answers together through a series of conversations. It took several years. Thankfully, I had time. Not everyone is that fortunate.

2. I am so glad my father was willing to meet with an eldercare attorney with me and we were able to take care of everything. There are some differences among states, but familiarize yourself with the following:

    Advance Directive or Living Will clearly states your end-of-life wishes.

    POLST (Physician Orders for Life-Sustaining Treatment)

    Durable Power of Attorney allows you to make financial and medical decisions if your parent becomes incapacitated.

Will gives you needed power after your parent is gone. Everyone "knows" how important a Will is, but if someone close to you dies without one, its importance increases instantly and dramatically.

3. Do whatever you can to get all siblings on board. This seems to range from easy and obvious to the challenge of a lifetime.

Chapter Two

THE SANDWICH GENERATION

A NEW DREAM FOR RETAILERS - ELDER CARE PRODUCTS

Marky writes

I looked in my Costco cart and realized that I was a walking advertisement for the Sandwich Generation. There was a huge box of diapers (I have my grandchildren over often and I take care of the youngest one day each week) and two huge boxes of Depends. I admit to hoping that no one would think the Depends were for me, ever-vain-caregiver-daughter that I am. But then I remembered that I come by it honestly: my mother was always fashionable and cared very much about how she looked. She exercised long before the term "workout" became the norm. In fact, I grew up watching my mother follow Jack LaLane on TV. Besides, there were coupons for both, so saving money won over my vanity.

My parents discovered Costco long before they moved closer to us after Mom's first stroke. They both loved it, especially my father. After they moved to an assisted living, I would drive over, load them in the accessible van and off we would go to Costco. Mom was wheelchair-bound for the last 5 years of her life, but her shopping instincts returned when she was let loose in Costco. I had many moments of panic, because she was fast and I couldn't see her above the counters.

My dad, on the other hand, loved the Costco mobility scooters but I could see him, because they have these little orange flags that stick way up in the air. I learned the hard way, NOT to plan to do any shopping for myself because just keeping track of them, getting them through the checkout and having a lunch of their favorite Costco hot dogs, loading them back in the van and getting them home was ENOUGH. They seemed to forget that they lived in a very small 2 bedroom apartment by this time. They still bought the large size or a case of everything. But they had fun. When I cleaned out my dad's apartment when we moved him to an adult family home, I found 3 cases of root beer, enough cereal for the entire building, boxes of dried up frozen cream puffs, MANY containers of vitamins, and enough toilet paper and bars of soap to last a lifetime. Sadly, they did.

The Sandwich Generation

On the day I rolled my Sandwich Generation cart up to the checkout line, I was by myself. I recognized an adult-child-of-an-elderly-parent in front of me. It's easy to recognize us. We're usually explaining something as we gently move an older person along, helping them navigate what must surely seem to be an overwhelming, fast, loud world to them. We also tend to look kind of weary. This adult child's mother was in the Costco mobility scooter (with the flag). The scooter basket was filled to the brim. I noticed two boxes of Depends. Then there was a regular cart, filled with cases of everything, just behind the mobility scooter. The adult daughter was paying for their haul.

Just as the cashier asked if they would like help out to their car, we all turned to see the mother fly off in the scooter, one hand on the steering wheel and one hand pulling their regular cart behind her, flag flying high. The cashier turned back and said,

Or maybe not! I hope I'm that feisty at her age.

I laughed so hard I confess to eyeing the Depends in my cart.

After Mom was gone, my dad continued to live another year in their assisted living facility. He missed her so much, but he had made friends there, played poker regularly when all of the guys could get upstairs and he loved the dining room. He also had a big screen TV, courtesy of Costco. But he was having trouble getting around, so I began researching mobility scooters, not to be confused with motorized wheelchairs. I can tell you that the world of scooters has blossomed into an industry that will rival cars before long. You can buy absolutely anything you want, from light and portable enough to qualify as a carry-on to one that looks like a miniature car, complete with windshield wipers. Since the-world-of-Craigslist had led us to an accessible van, I figured we could find a good scooter. We did. My dad loved it. I remember the first time we went to town to get his hair cut, me walking and my dad gleefully scootering along, his independence restored. It was about 6 blocks.

Five years earlier, when I had decided to take Mom for a "walk" around their apartment, she was still in a manual wheelchair. I had somehow missed the fact that they lived on a hill. I got to the end of the driveway and turned her chair toward town. Mom was never a big person, but she had gained weight being in the chair and I panicked as I envisioned her chair careening down the hill. I instantly realized this wasn't a hill, but a *mountain*. All I could do was frantically push her straight across the street, beg for help for a passerby and return to the parking lot of their building. That was the extent of that walk.

But my dad's scooter had power and I figured we would be okay. All things considered, the outing was a success in spite of the fact that for some reason, my dad left the barber shop in reverse and backed right over the curb. The barber and I saved him and returned him to the sidewalk.

After 7 years of caring for my parents, I have become an expert of sorts in the field of eldercare products. I can find the best price on a mobilized scooter, wheelchair, people who repair them, batteries, Depends, catheter equipment, walkers, walking canes with cool heads, special drinking cups, eating utensils, hearing aids, bed rails, shower seats, toilet seat risers and an endless list of things I had never heard of. But necessities have a way of demanding attention and shortening the learning curve.

Humor helps. Coupons help. And when I see those other adult children in Costco, I look them in the eye and thank them. I can no longer take my dad to Costco and I miss watching the little orange flag fly across the great box store. And I realize that there, if God is gracious, will go us.

Are Sandwiches Good for Us?

Dawna writes

I've always loved double decker sandwiches more than most people. I have the mid-section to prove that claim. What's not to love? When I was growing up Mom fell into a pattern (Okay, maybe it was a rut) of serving the same thing on certain days of the week. Monday night was my favorite. We had BLT sandwiches. Two deckers of bacon, lettuce and tomatoes; I was in heaven.

Today there is a local sandwich shop where I occasionally treat myself to a #34. That is a corned beef and swiss cheese double decker, yum. And lately there has been a chili parlor in our Cincinnati area which has been advertising *quadruple* decker sandwiches. Four layers. On the TV commercials these sandwiches look HUGE, impossible to maneuver and consume. I can't imagine getting my mouth around one of those, but they are great to fantasize about.

Impossible or not, my life has been like that outrageous quadruple layered sandwich for a long time. It looks idyllic and delicious in the photograph, but in reality it is unbelievably hard to maneuver or digest. As I write this my family has had four generations alive for twenty-two years. While medical science can extend our lives, who is caring for the people in the middle of that sandwich? I know the answer because I have lived it. No one.

Life is a series of mental snapshots. A couple of the most stressful moments that are imprinted into my mind I'm going to describe. These are moments of such heightened stress and emotion I can visualize them right down to the smallest detail and know they will never leave my mind. But at the time they took place I don't even know if anyone else was aware of them. I didn't have time to ask a friend for help. It seems like the times when we need our friends the most, we don't even have a moment or the emotional energy to access them.

In the first scene I see myself with a twelve-year-old daughter who had special needs. She was in junior high and struggling academically and socially. Junior High is when friends start excluding others with any differences. She needed my help with her school work every night. After teaching all day (working with high school age students who were described as 'at risk'), I would come home and spend two hours per night next to my daughter at the kitchen table reading her assignments to her and then paraphrasing them so she could comprehend them. We're not talking about a mom who fixed dinner while her daughter did her homework. We're talking about my sitting next to her and explaining every single concept and then watching carefully as she wrote her responses.

But wait. My other daughter was a single mom at the time. She was in college. I was paying for her tuition and daytime child care for her son with my teacher's salary. In the evenings she was working while I was taking care of her one-year-old son, my first treasured grandson. I would rock him in his infant seat with my foot as I helped my younger daughter with special needs. I will never forget the seemingly endless pressure and hopelessness I felt in that moment. It is as though I am having an out of body experience hovering over the top of that table and looking down at my pitiful self. I cannot believe I lived through it. I don't even remember talking to a friend about it. I didn't have the time. My mom was walking miles a day for exercise in the local shopping mall at this time. She couldn't understand why I wouldn't walk with her.

Another scene forever branded in my mind was when my mother was in a nursing home for the first time. It was a temporary stay which lasted for about a month for rehabilitation following a fall in which her leg was broken near the knee and she had surgery for repairs. Mom didn't like being in the nursing home, even though she chose the one she wanted, they were wonderful to her, and provided the rehabilitation she needed at the time.

She was laying on the guilt like a thick layer of mayonnaise on that quadruple decker sandwich. I was still teaching full time and had a sixteen-year-old daughter about whom I was worried. This daughter had battled brain cancer at age five and I had a suspicion that the cancer had returned. I had ordered an unscheduled MRI just four months earlier to relieve my suspicions. It showed nothing. But those suspicions still clawed at me.

Mom demanded daily visits to the nursing home. Did I mention I was also doing her laundry? Soon her stay there would be over. I'll never forget a phone call my mom made to me on a Wednesday. Does it tell you something that I still know the day of the week that I received that call? Mom's voice was quite aggravated as she demanded.

> *Dauna, my physical therapist wants to know what time I will be picked up on Friday, who will be driving the car and what kind of a car they will be driving. I keep asking you for this information, but you won't make the plans. I need to know these things NOW!*

I replied with annoyance

> *Gee, I don't know yet, Mom. Between now and then I have to figure out if my daughter's cancer is back. I'll get back to you.*

It might have been the first time I was ever really curt to my mom (but not the last). Sure enough, on Thursday my daughter was re-diagnosed with cancer. But I had my mom's plans in place so she could get home from the nursing home on Friday. My sixteen-year-old daughter only lived another four months. So you can only imagine what those months were like. My mom is still alive and living in her own home more than twelve years later.

How did I survive all this? *I don't know.* Who takes care of this generation sandwiched in the middle? I don't think anyone is doing it well enough. It seems to be up to us. We have got to somehow, *on purpose*, release ourselves from some of the guilt of trying to be everything for everybody. We've got to lean on our friends for support. Talk to them about what we're experiencing. Accept help when it is offered. Ask for help when it isn't offered. Demand help when others are reluctant. Where are the agencies and systems to support us? In the final analysis it is a family problem, a challenge each of us has to maneuver in our own way.

Do as I say and not as I do. I'm writing this in the middle of the night. Why? I'll be giving my mom a shampoo and blow dry in her home this morning before I go to my granddaughter's dance competition in the afternoon. I'll be helping my daughter who will be at another granddaughter's gymnastics meet.

I love it all. I'm grateful for it all. I promise I am. But sometimes there are some really tough pickles and even some rotten things right in the middle of that four-decker sandwich. We must help one another. That's one reason I jumped on board when my friend, Marky, suggested we share our experiences about helping our aging parents in writing. I hope others can relate to what I'm describing, and find some hope and encouragement between the sentences.

I'm surviving. Most days I'm even thriving. But some days I not only *want* to cry, I *do* cry. These are not just empty words when I say them to you.

I honestly know what you are going through.

I hope my experiences will help you find your path through this challenging time in your life. When my parents are no longer on this earth I want to look back and be able to believe…

I'm proud of the job I've done.

I also don't want to beat myself to death with guilt in the meantime. Is it possible? I think so. I hope we can help you feel that way too.

Tips for the Sandwich Generation

Dawna Says

1. Have conversations with others who are caring for their aging parents. Listen and learn. This topic brings all of us together. Many of your co-workers or acquaintances may be experiencing your same dilemmas. Ask them.

2. Look for help. Ask for help. Accept help. If necessary demand help. This is no time for an 'I can handle it all myself' attitude.

3. Important DISCOVERY I made: My mother is nicer to everyone in the world than she is to me. I'm her rock and whipping post. She doesn't have a spouse and therefore leans on me more. She is confident I will love her in spite of it all.

4. Therefore, it is important to set limits when a parent controls a child with guilt. You will need to decide what your personal limits are. Discuss them with someone who knows the situation. Then stand by those limits. Otherwise you won't be able to stay the course for the long run.

5. When I asked a friend to sit with Mom at the hospital, I felt guilty. But Mom was very sweet to her. It relieved my sense of guilt for asking for help. Result? I got to see my grandson make a touchdown. Mom *had* to act nicer. My friend understood my situation better. In my book that is a win/win/win.

Marky says

1. At some point, I realized that I had no idea what the Sandwich Generation meant. That is because beyond the obvious, every situation is different. Family dynamics are powerful, deeply rooted and often the opposite of the warm, fuzzy feeling of the word family. Researching and talking with others is a start. But in the end, you'll need to listen, observe and intuit your own family dynamics. Then talk. Then make decisions. Then let the guilt go.

2. There are a number of credible and worthy websites where you can find information about all aspects of caring for elderly parents. Here are a few that I have found to be interesting and informative:

    1. www.SageMinder.com

    2. www.MaturityMatters.net

    3. New York Times – The New Old Age Blog

Chapter Three

SENIORS VS. SENIORS

THE DAY THE SENIORS COLLIDED

Marky writes

I had been teaching high school seniors for many years. Long enough that when people asked *how can you spend entire days with teenagers?* I felt kind of sorry for them...I really enjoyed the kids. Most high school teachers ride the wave of energy, passion and somehow learn to navigate the collision between maturity and immaturity that governed our days. My daughter gave me some advice when I began teaching:

Never walk around with lipstick on your teeth.

Don't get yourself on a talk show.

I took her advice seriously because she was a recent high school graduate, so I figured she should know important stuff. I did my best to dress somewhat fashionably. I didn't worry too much about the talk show part-I was old enough to be the grandmother to the boys in my classes and I had learned how to connect with them through humor. I had been teaching junior English and senior public speaking for 6 years and I was one of two senior class advisors. The job description of senior class advisor was to guide them as they made prom, senior picnic and graduation plans. In reality, that meant learning how to quell the rising tide of emotion and desperation as they neared the end, many realizing that they had left a few things undone, such as major assignments, planning for college, applying for college, maturing, etc. Of course, the seniors were expected to plan the details of their events, but as the dominoes began to fall, we often picked up the pieces to save our own sanity. Necessary details were left to the senior advisors and a committee of other teachers, all of us attempting to keep our respective classes under control and possibly learning.

I coped with all of this reasonably well for about 7 years, until my mother had her first stroke. My parents moved closer to me and settled into an assisted living facility. My father transported my mother to her monthly appointment with the urologist. She was wheel-chair bound and dependent on a permanent catheter.

SENIORS VS. SENIORS

That's when the seniors began colliding. The sense of balance, orderliness and control in my life was to be challenged many times.

June 6th~The Day the Seniors Collided ~was the most demanding day of being a high school senior advisor. It was the day before graduation (our seniors graduated at Safeco Baseball Field-a TRUE EVENT) and the senior picnic was that afternoon with yearbook distribution. My juniors were particularly stressed about their final. My phone rang. It was an EMP, calling from the urologist's office where my father had taken my mother for her monthly catheter change. My father had passed out and *which hospital did I want them to take him to?* In my how-can-this-happen-today-state, I told him the wrong hospital. This situation required two people-one to see to my father and one to pick up my mother in the accessible van. My husband chose to meet my dad at the hospital and since I had not yet realized I told the EMP the wrong hospital, my husband went to the "regular" hospital. I had to leave my advisor partner with the seniors, find a sub for my juniors and rescue my mother as soon as I could.

My husband eventually found my dad and took him home that evening with a *let's just watch this* diagnosis. This was to be the beginning of a two year fight over my dad's driving. I don't think the seniors even missed me in their heightened state of euphoria and I was able to get my mother home in time for her nap.

The Day the Seniors Collided was to become one of many I was to face in the seven years of caring for my parents. My mantra when I left for school was to leave my personal problems at home during the day because I needed all my energy- and my wits- to meander successfully through a day of teaching high school. I would show up at 7:00 every weekday morning and I was prepared for the day. I'm a high-energy person and I enjoyed a true passion for my job, the curriculum and the kids. I loved it. I often checked the little mirror my daughter had given me for any suspect lipstick and I kept off myself off the talk show circuit. But always, in my pocket, was my cell phone.

On vibrate.

Can You Speak Senior?
Dawna writes

I've spent many years teaching high school seniors. It has been an incredible honor to share one of the most memorable and poignant years of a young person's life with them. I've gotten to view all the senior pictures, help them select a university, and watch them walk across the stage in their caps and gowns.

But along the way I had to learn to speak "senior," a language I didn't learn as I prepared to teach high school. Let me give you some examples.

When they say…

> Mizz E. I can't like believe this. She like just looked like right at me and then like turned around and walked away like she was like better than me or something.

It really means

Two girls are having a disagreement and if I don't diffuse it soon, pandemonium will ensue.

Or

> *Mizz E. You be tripping?*

Really means…

This is way too much homework! Don't you realize I have football conditioning before school and football practice after school this time of year?

But what made this new language all the more confusing was that I had to learn to speak another kind of "senior" simultaneously. I had to learn to speak 'senior citizen' at the same time I was learning to communicate with high school seniors. Here is what I have learned so far.

When Mom says,

> *Binky is almost out of cat food. Could you just pick up six cans at the discount store for me?*

She really means…

> *No matter how inconvenient it is for you with your two kids, five grandchildren and full time job, get me six cans of cat food <u>today</u> that cost 29 cents each. Get the kind Binky likes.*

Solution (and it took us many years of trial and error to figure out these solutions so they are really quite valuable). You may use this knowledge for free. What a bargain!

Get a case of Binky's favorite cat food and carry it in your vehicle. Pay any price you have to. Dole it out to Grandma in just the amount she asks for and lie and say you bought it at the discount store for 29 cents per can. It is the only solution. Binky won't eat the cheap stuff.

When you arrive at Grandma's house it is a complete certainty that she will *then* say

> *Binky needs kitty litter now.*

Grin to yourself as you pull the kitty litter from the car. She will comment

> *Oh, I didn't need that now. My social security check doesn't come in until next week.*

Cover your mouth and nose with your scarf so the cat…uh…fumes don't knock you over. Drag the kitty litter into the house. (You are only allowed to purchase the 100 pound bag because it saves a few pennies.) Tell Grandma not to worry she can pay you next week. She'll forget, but that's OK. Oh, and you'll have to change the kitty litter box also whether you have a life threatening cat allergy or not. Just ask my daughter.

But don't ever start feeling clever, because it is guaranteed that as you leave Grandma's house she will definitely tell you something else she needs. This rule always applies whether you have delivered one or one thousand items. It is a law of the universe.

When Grandma says

> *I've got to get busy shopping for Christmas.*

She really means…

Come to my house and pick up the $15.00 I have budgeted for each of your family members. Shop for all of your brood. Bring the gifts to me for approval. Buy several options because often Grandma will say,

> *Oh, I don't want to give her that.*

If you don't have a second option, it is back to the store for you. It doesn't matter that troll dolls are in and it is all your kid wants. If Grandma doesn't like the look of the troll, she's not letting you write her name on the gift tag. Once you have received her approval, it is then up to you to wrap the gift and deliver it.

When Grandma says

> *I wish I knew where that door decoration is.*

She really means…

Go out to the garage and go through every box you can find. Bring her anything that looks like it might pass for a door decoration for any season. You will never find the right one, so don't beat yourself up unnecessarily. Just get dusty and sweaty enough so that she knows you were making a real effort. When you finally give up she will say

> *You know, I think I gave that door decoration to Goodwill last year.*

You can swear if you have to. She won't hear you.

While I was teaching future teachers, one of my jobs was to teach the stages of child development. I carefully explained to teens and young adults that it was completely developmentally appropriate for a toddler to be self-centered. They are focused only on themselves. Toddlers who *can't* share *aren't* selfish, they are simply toddlers acting exactly like toddlers are supposed to act. They will slowly grow out of it as they enter the next stage of development. They will eventually learn to share and care about what others think.

Sometimes the resemblance between senior citizens and toddlers is just a little too freaky. Is this what we become? Grandma has no interest in your workload, how many of your kids are home sick, whether the road is icy or the fact that you are having a personal meltdown. She will give you her grocery list no matter what your circumstances and remind you to get each item on her list at a separate store to save money.

In some ways it is comforting to at least know the rules. The sun comes up in the morning. The sun goes down at night. Grandma will always have a list of things for you to do for her. I've done the best I can do for you. I have told you the rules. The rest is up to you.

Tips for Talking with Seniors

Dawna says

1. You'll have to know your parent to figure out what they really want. My mom uses lists of chores to keep her children coming around. Sometimes it works in the opposite way, but she doesn't understand that.

2. I have to squelch my guilt whenever I walk away because she will *always* have something more on her list. That

means I will always feel guilty leaving her. Frankly I hate that but it is something I have had to learn to deal with. Walking away feeling guilty.

3. Many of her "lists" mean she just wants you to visit. Read between the lines.

4. I have to be patient when talking with Mom on the phone. Since she doesn't drive anymore, her life doesn't change as much. Many of her stories are repeats. On my patient days I can listen to a story for the twentieth time. On my bad days I sometimes cut her off and then feel guilty. On those days my daughter listens to me and understands. She loves Grandma too. She helps relieve me of my guilt.

5. Talking with my dad is entirely different from talking with my mother. If he has something on his mind, he may show up and talk about his car or your car. He doesn't discuss feelings or fears much.

6. However, if I am distraught, I have to hide it from my mom. She's a worrier. I know however, I can dump my fears on my dad. He can handle them. *Even at age 88 he can still play that role with me.* It is refreshing not to have to be so strong. Writing these tips has helped me put that into words.

Marky says

1. At this point, I was learning the precarious business of balancing my life with the needs of my parents. There is no easy answer here, but I think I had an innate ability to

set boundaries which allowed me to say no without guilt marching in.

2. I also realized that while my husband and my married daughters loved my parents, no one-absolutely no one- is on the front line with adult children.

3. My son-in-law encouraged me to join a support group. I thought it was a great idea and I would have, if I had had time. But I did talk with peers, researched where I could and became verbally and sincerely appreciative toward my parents' caregivers.

Chapter Four

ELDER NEEDS

WALKERS, GRABBERS, REACHERS, CARTS AND OTHER UFOS

Dawna writes

I remember the moment well. All Mom's kids, a couple spouses and grandkids were sitting in the surgery waiting area. Mom was in surgery having a broken leg repaired. She was seventy-six years old and had been standing on top of a kitchen chair changing a light bulb when she lost her balance and fell. She lay there for a couple of moments assessing the situation. She was able to scoot to the kitchen phone and call me. She wasn't sure if she was really hurt, but thought so.

I quickly drove the twenty minutes to her house. Meanwhile she had to 'butt walk' from the kitchen, through the utility room to remove the chain from the back door so I could get in. As soon as I saw her leg, I knew it was time to call an ambulance. She spent the time while we waited for the emergency vehicle lamenting about how no one would ever help her change a light bulb. Mom never misses any opportunity to dish out guilt. It's probably her best, most effective recipe.

Now we were waiting to hear what the surgeon had to say following the surgery. His report did nothing to reassure us.

> *The break was ugly. I had to use some pins, and a plate to make the repair. It doesn't help that it was close to the knee.*

"What kind of recovery will she need, doctor?" I asked.

> *She'll need at least a month to six weeks in a good nursing home that provides daily physical therapy. Then she'll need someone to care for her in her home (or in their home) for a while longer. With this kind of a break she may never walk without a walker again.*

When he walked away we all sat there stunned. He had just said two different things that every one of us knew Mom would abhor. The man had the audacity to say 'nursing home' and 'never walk without a walker again' in the same paragraph. Then he just walked out of the room like he hadn't just dropped the atom bomb.

We just sat in silence and looked at each other. At that time Mom was walking from three to five miles per day with her mall walking buddies. She'd spent her whole life saying she would never live in a nursing home. When we had recovered just a little from our shock, someone asked the obvious question.

Who is gonna' tell her she's gotta' go into a nursing home?

Every finger in the room but mine pointed to me. I gulped.

Then someone said,

Who in the world is going to tell her she is going to be using a walker for the rest of her life?

We **all** agreed on that answer. No one would tell her. And we didn't. Ever.

The good news is Mom did recover from that surgery. Sure, she had to use a walker for a while to learn to walk again. But she was able to get rid of the walker after a while. I think it was because of the strength she had built up in the muscles of her legs with all her daily walking. She eventually returned to her walking buddies. But unlike before she had to sit down between laps sometimes and she couldn't walk as far.

But that accident signaled the beginning of the downward slide. We learned about walkers, reachers, commode seats that made toilets higher, gizmos that helped you put your socks on, long handled foot horns, and elastic shoe laces, to name just a few.

Within a few years mom bought a shiny red walker that had a seat. We could still go shopping and to craft shows and she could rest when necessary. She bragged to everyone about how handy her walker was. By then she didn't just tolerate the walker, she was proud of it. But there came the day when she even used the walker in her home and we began to avoid large stores that didn't have electric carts.

Mom dreamed about having her own battery operated electric cart. She fell for a commercial that showed senior citizens driving down the road with their electric carts that had those tall flags flying in the air. I think she thought she could drive out of town with one. I was more skeptical. I own an SUV and I knew it wouldn't fit into my car. She was certain I should put a carrier on the back of my car. But that would prevent me from opening my back hatch. I also knew I couldn't lift a motorized cart. I was less than enthusiastic about these plans. She did, finally get a motorized cart. She uses it a little around the house, but also some times when my daughter takes her out. My daughter has five children and thus a van almost the size of a small school bus. She is also young enough to lift that contraption in and out of the car without a mechanical lift.

Mom is always talking to store management about their needs for electric carts. She hunts them down like prey and gives them an impassioned speech. Some of them recognize her and try their best to hide. It embarrasses me and I often just walk away. I suppose I'll only appreciate it when I begin to need electric carts and there is a row of shiny ones all lined up in the front of every store. I'll have to mentally thank Mom every time I climb on board.

Recently when I was visiting Mom she complained to me (with a twinkle in her eye) about something my daughter, Jodi, had done. Spotting an advertisement, Jodi had sent off for a free sample of a Depends-type disposable undergarment. My mom isn't a small woman and the offer was for a 'plus size' disposable undergarment for incontinence.

The free sample arrived in a cardboard container that was open and the contents were hanging halfway out. Mom lamented about the across-the-street male minister neighbor who carries her mail from the roadside mailbox to prop inside her storm door each day. Mom thought he might have been scandalized or worse…believed mom was that big! Then she stretched the item out on the floor with indignation. She used her reacher to spread it out completely. We collapsed in laughter. Truly it seemed the size of one of those giant aircrafts that carry tanks to the war zone. It had to be the size designed for those huge suma wrestlers. Hysteria overtook us. We just could *not* stop laughing.

I called Jodi still giggling and she drove over for a viewing with a couple of her children in tow. The grandchildren were puzzled and said so.

What in the world is that?

Four generations were laughing so hard together that the contagion wouldn't quit. When one person would regain control, two more would collapse in mirth. We laughed so hard and so long that Jodi herself thought she would be a candidate for incontinence garments.

There have been many moments caring for mom when the difficult, scary or even sad events held power over all of us. It was refreshing to share a great laugh together. Every person of the four generations bearing witness that day will remember that moment forever. And then they'll undoubtedly laugh all over again.

The Shadows of Aging

Marky writes

My first conscious memory of walkers was having dinner with my parents shortly after they moved to a continuing care retirement community near Lacey, WA. The in-house restaurant offered a nice place for residents to entertain visiting family… and surrounding the fireplace was a parking lot for walkers. Mom had suffered a second stroke and was using a walker, temporarily she constantly reminded us. Her goal, at 84, was to get back on the golf course. She loved all of her doctors and therapists, but the only thing she ever said to them was,

> *When can I get back on the golf course?*

Mom never returned to the golf course, but she never stopped planning. She would even order new golf clothes each spring. She was to live 5 more years, most of that time being wheelchair-bound. The true meaning of that description was to become painfully real to me. Often, in my dreams, my mother would walk again. Then I would wake up and return to the world of lifts, bedrails, catheters, swollen ankles and the fear of pressure sores that would not heal. As with many changes, you gradually absorb a new way of life and the early I-can't-live-this-way horror becomes a new normal.

Not too long after my parents moved to a home in the retirement community about two hours from my husband and me,

Mom suffered a debilitating stroke that left her unable to bear weight. That means wheel-chair-bound. Life becomes centered on daily activities that become mountains to climb all day. Mom needed a catheter, which required monthly changes. But getting her to the doctor meant finding one who could lift her onto the table. This also meant purchasing an accessible van to take her to appointments.

At that point, my parents moved to an assisted living facility fairly close to us. My dad was still able to take her to appointments and after many fruitless phone calls, I was able to find a new doctor and a urologist who could take care of Mom. Slowly, she adjusted to the catheter and my dad purchased a lift for the caregivers to move her from her chair to the bed and shower-and oh yes-the rolling toilet. I could put Mom in the lift, but it was a new learning curve each time.

Are you ready, Mom?

I think so…

I mean, is the belt in the right place?

I'm not sure…

I was never to recover from the time Mom slipped out of the lift when I happened to be visiting. Though I held my breath each time, thankfully, she never slipped out again. Enough other crises happened that the lift became the least of my worries.

There was the time she leaned over to pick something up, fell out of her wheel chair and broke her leg badly enough to require a pin. After 2 months in a skilled nursing facility, she returned home and the first time the caregiver used her lift, I realized the belt held her just where the pin was in her leg. Mom didn't worry about it. I did.

There was the time my dad took her to her monthly appointment and he himself passed out in the doctor's office. My husband and I both left work, one to rescue Mom and the other to the hospital with my dad.

Since Mom was not able to move her wheelchair, we decided she needed an electric chair. Naturally, that gave her mobility and a sense of independence, but it also meant losing more muscle mass. We were indoctrinated into the world of battery-dependence, new-best-friend-repairmen and walls and doors with scrapes and black marks.

My very independent mother, who *still* thought she would be able to play golf was gradually letting go of life. I was to grieve the loss of my mother long before she died. We did find things to laugh about, though, like the many times I realized that her catheter bag needed to be emptied NOW. Finding a restroom and emptying the bag, I laughed and told her she could pee just like a guy! She laughed hilariously. It was so wonderful to hear my sweet mother laugh.

My father was determined to return to the life they had always enjoyed. He never accepted aging and was never to accept my mother's death, even two years later. After Mom died, my dad gave away the walker, the wheelchair, the lift and even sold the accessible van. I actually searched out the person he gave the wheelchair to and begged to have it back. It was expensive and I knew what was coming. The last time my dad went to an Oregon State Football game with my brother and his grandsons-in-law, he gratefully accepted the wheelchair. Walking to the stadium had changed a lot since my parents were there in the 1940s.

At some point during the last 5 years of my mother's life, my dad began to show obvious signs of aging. As a baby step on the way to a walker, which he wouldn't even discuss, I began a cane-campaign. Since my dad had enjoyed many hobbies, I figured that if a cane reflected one of his loves, he would accept it. He said no. I ordered a beautiful cane, its handle a carved fish. Very uptown, I thought. He still said no. I took it when we went to the dining room in his assisted living facility for lunch, casually hanging it on his chair. Bill noticed the fish handle…Bingo! The cane became cool and my dad adjusted until it was as necessary to him as a woman's purse is to her. My dad can no longer use his cane. It has a place of honor in my memory and in my home.

After I was finally able to get my father's car keys for good (not an enjoyable process) I realized that if I could find a mobility scooter he would regain some sense of independence. I found a shiny gold mobility scooter that my dad loved. He insisted on riding it even up to the dining room, sabotaging his ongoing need for exercise. I decided to ignore that battle. I had won the car keys, after all. He absolutely loved that scooter. I will always treasure the day we "walked" to town to get his hair cut. It was a mile walk, a fun, daily habit for me. For my father, it was almost a return to an earlier self, flying in Korea, piloting his boat, absolute freedom. It was to be a short-lived return to independence. He suffered a debilitating stroke several months later, leaving him wheelchair-bound.

This time around, an electric chair was not an option. My father's mind and left side were permanently affected and the Adult Family Home did not allow electric chairs or scooters. We had donated Mom's lift when she died, feeling liberated that we would never need one again. My father's needs were even more pronounced than my mother's had been. This time, we needed an electric lift. Battery worries and a life dependent upon mechanical means returned to steal my peace of mind. My father has so little left beyond a strong will to live. His dementia has robbed me of his presence in so many ways. But it also wraps him in the cocoon of his very small world, unaware of so much loss. He still knows us and often tells us.

> *Your mom was here last night. My answer? Please give her my love when you talk with her tonight.*

Tips for Elder Needs

Dawna says

1. Look for medical supply stores. You'll find things to help you that you never have seen. They had the solution to many of our challenges.

2. There is a mom and pop pharmacy in my mom's town that is much better equipped with rental medical equipment than any national chain. Don't overlook the mom and pop drugstores.

3. If you can accompany your parent to occupational or physical therapy appointments, the therapist is a wonderful resource for ideas to help your parent. Ask them questions.

Marky says

1. Do research online for whatever equipment or supplies you need. I just googled the needed item and the sources were endless. I had far more success online that I did when visiting local medical supply stores.

2. Craigslist is a valuable resource for larger items and we were very successful here. If shipping is possible, check Ebay.

3. Local Senior Centers are often a great source for free or very reasonable equipment. They often loan items as well.

Chapter Five

SAFETY ISSUES

Don't Worry Your Mother

Dauna writes

"Don't worry your mother." That was one of my dad's mantras. Mom said the same thing.

> *Dauna, you know how I worry. I just can't help it, I worry. You don't know what it's like to be a worrier. You don't even have a healthy sense of fear. Don't scare me!*

The problem is everything scares her. Notice how all the responsibility for this worry is shifted onto someone else?

My mother gasps when anything scares or concerns her…or even if she remembers something suddenly. It is a fast intake of breath that most people would only use in the instant before they realized they were going to run over a small child who had just darted into the roadway. I'll be driving along and mom will suddenly gasp loudly and sometimes even put her hand to her chest. My instinct is to slam on my brakes and look for a dead person under my wheels as my arm instinctively extends to protect Mom from going through the windshield on impact. Then she'll say something like,

I forgot to call Jerry back.

I want to press a seat eject button and catapult her into the air. I have complained about her gasping over minor issues a thousand times. The gasps continue.

I was not a kid who would worry her mother. I was a completely straight arrow. I was always where I said I would be and never late arriving home. I didn't do any underage drinking, smoke, do drugs, nor run with people who did. I was, however, independent. I could live alone without fear, travel by plane, and drive anywhere. All of her children "caused her to worry" by becoming independent. We were thoughtless that way. When I began traveling the country for speaking engagements she started watching the news channels for planes that went down and living in terror any time I was out of town. I stopped telling her when I would travel. She still calls me and reports any plane crash.

When my parents separated for the final time and actually *did* go through with a divorce, my mother was fifty-one years old. Mom and Dad had been separated several times while we kids were in the house; but in her fifties mom had to learn to live alone. She now has been living alone for thirty-seven years and has been retired for twenty-four, not bad for a gasping worrier.

But there were challenges along the way. Even though she has an unlisted phone number, she received repeated prank calls at night which terrified her. While fearless people just hang up, 'a worrier' will listen to a comment or two and I'm certain, express fear, so the prankster would call repeatedly. We finally had to get the police involved. They went to the home of the offender. It was a kid making calls without the parents being aware. The kid denied, the father denied, the police showed the phone records and spelled out the consequences of any further calls. The calls stopped. But for a while Mom was afraid the caller would come to her house to get her.

Once Mom broke her leg and lay on the floor thinking about how to reach us, we had her get a life alert button that she wears twenty-four hours a day. She can even fall just outside her home (which she has done more than once) and the life alert button will call all of us kids. Sometimes Mom looks upon these life alert occasions as social events. When Mom falls she can no longer get up on her own unless there is a firm piece of furniture nearby. Once I arrived first to help her up. She wouldn't let me help.

No, wait until Daryl arrives.

Daryl sent my niece and her boyfriend. Mom was embarrassed to have the boyfriend help lift her so she said

Wait and see if Jodi comes.

Five people had to arrive before she would let any of us try to stand her up, something I could have done on my own with a firm piece of furniture. Each time someone arrived mom would say,

> *What did they say when they called you? Who else did they call? What did that person say?*

Mom loves to be center of attention. She wants all of her children to run toward her demonstrating concern. She takes attendance at these events. (Disclaimer: When I read this to her, she denied it. But it is an opinion shared by the rest of the family. All of them.)

Occasionally I will kind of review safety rules with Mom. She has a chain on one door but a deadbolt we can open with a key on another. That way if she is down and can't get up, we can still get to her to help. She carries a portable phone on her walker. She knows not to open the door without looking to see who is there.

But recently she slipped up. A local woman who is a drug addict knocked on Mom's door late at night. She is the ex-wife of one of my brother's friends. She has been incarcerated for drug issues, but Mom didn't know this. Her latest gimmick for acquiring drug money is to knock on the doors of the elderly parents of her former friends. She banged on Mom's door late at night. Mom opened the chain 'because it was a woman'. She told Mom who she was. Mom barely remembered her name. But parents from my mother's generation are always polite. The woman claimed her ninety-year-old mother was in the hospital and she wanted to go see her but her car was broken down.

Mom was somewhat confused about what she wanted.

I don't know how I can help you. My car isn't here.

Thank goodness that was true or Mom probably would have given her the keys. Then the lady asked for money. Mom left the door and went to get $20.00 out of her purse. Fortunately the woman didn't follow her in. Mom gave her the money and the addict left.

The next day she realized all her mistakes and called me to confess. I called the police. They were well aware of the woman. She has done this to many people throughout the community. She knows just what to say and how to get money without technically breaking any laws.

It was scary at the time. But in hindsight it was another good lesson. We were afraid she might come back, but the policeman said she rarely did. If she did come back Mom was to tell her not to ever come on her property again and call the police. Then if she came back they could do something about it. Scams today are changing and evolving quickly. We've even had two instances of Mom shopping for groceries in a store's electric cart when a man approached her and offered to get something off a shelf for which Mom was reaching. He will start an innocuous conversation, just vague pleasantries. Mom doesn't pay much attention; she is price checking. Then his conversation branches into suggestive areas.

Your hair is beautiful. I know what you <u>really</u> come here for.

Mom will say

My daughter is in the next aisle and I need to talk to her.

Then she hits her accelerator button and scoots away. When we question Mom on his appearance she says

> *You don't expect me to look at him, do you? I don't want to look at him.*

This has happened twice in two different national chain stores- once when mom was with my daughter and once when she was with me. The first time we reported it to the store manager. The second time we were in too big of a hurry to take the time. But I do know there is a guy in our area who is targeting senior women in stores. What a creep.

My mom has come a long way. So have we. She wants to live in her home. The choice always seems to come down to freedom or fear. Growing up Mom seemed the least likely candidate to choose freedom over fear. But she has and I'm proud of her.

Two Funnies

I like the way this last story flows and I didn't want to change or lengthen it. But I just have to share two funny background stories.

With five children my daughter, Jodi has to sandwich her grandma in at odd moments. Often she gives Grandma very short notice.

> *I'm in my car on the way, Grandma, get ready quickly.*

Grandma uses a walker, a grabber, and lots of other gizmos to get ready. This is not a fast process. On the day that the store creep first approached Grandma she had a case of particularly outrageous bed head. Jodi was a little embarrassed about it, but didn't want to hurt Grandma's feelings so she didn't say anything about it.

In the store, Grandma said to Jodi

> *This sounds totally weird, but I think there was some guy coming on to me or something. He told me I had beautiful hair and said he knew what I <u>really</u> wanted.*

Jodi replied

> *Well, Grandma, I think you've got it right, because if he told you your hair is beautiful today, something is really fishy about this.*

Another time my friend Bonnie and I were having dinner at a local family restaurant. One of us had just told a funny story and we were laughing heartily. Some seemingly friendly guy walked past our booth and just said in passing

> *Well, you gals look like you are having a great time, but I know what you <u>really</u> want.*

We were still in the midst of our laughter but after we finished laughing Bonnie looked at me and said,

> *What did that guy just say?*

I said,

> *I think he said he knows what we <u>really</u> want.*

Maybe it was because we had already been laughing but we just collapsed in laughter all over again. When I could finally speak I said

Oh no. I think that might have been Grandma's 'creepy guy'. That is exactly what he says to her. Oh God. Does that mean we are elderly women?

More hysterical laughter.

Neither one of us had a clue what he looked like. We were no better than Grandma at identifying him.

Protecting My Parents: Batteries, Fraud and Bed Rails

Marky writes

Hindsight. If ever one could benefit from knowing issues ahead of time, it's when you take care of an elderly parent. I would have thought their overall health would be the controlling factor and certainly it was in many ways. As their physical and mental health began to deteriorate, though, the edges and repercussions of health issues began to take center stage of my life. Pills went a long way toward controlling blood pressure, arrhythmic hearts, infections and mental stability. But an entirely new world of needs began to seep into my days: batteries that hadn't been re-charged or that wore out and weren't easily available, suspect charges on credit cards, a growing mountain of solicitations and promises in the mail and on the phone, and, later, laws against bed rails that were needed to keep wondering minds and bodies safely in bed at night.

I was first introduced to life-dependent-upon-batteries when we decided my mother needed an electric wheelchair. The decision presented a trade-off. The independence Mom gained would be countered by weakened muscles. Even though I encouraged her mantra-dream, *I plan to be back on the golf course*, I knew my dad needed respite from answering Mom's every need of movement.

We bought an electric wheelchair. One battery is not enough-you need a backup, and they're expensive. Mom's new-found independence was mechanically dependent. I had the repair company on speed dial. I was forever thanking people for doing their job. Her lift, though not battery-dependent, needed service at one point. I begged shamelessly for quick service. The wheelchair van needed the ordinary repairs of any car, but its importance increased dramatically when I drove it. Getting it in for maintenance required an intricate dance of pickups, drop-offs and scheduling of at least 3 family members. And, thanks to the cat, Nellie the Terrorist, all of this was complicated when she ate the foam handles from wheelchairs, walkers and the lift.

When my father had the stroke that left him wheelchair bound, I was able to find an electric lift for his caregivers. This is a godsend piece of equipment for someone who needs it, but it requires batteries. Very expensive batteries. My father begged for an electric wheelchair, but the rules of the skilled nursing facility and the adult family home wouldn't allow that. Truthfully, he would not have been able to maneuver the chair, which he saw as his last touch with independence. My father, the pilot of 1600 hours in B-24 and B-26 airplanes, both nicknamed *The Widowmaker* was to end his days in a manual wheelchair. I signed 4 documents to make sure he had a bedrail. Two of those where required and two I created. As my dad's dementia increased, his ability to assess his remaining skills decreased, scaring his caregivers and me. After he fell out of his bed and was taken to emergency, I demanded a bedrail.

When my parents moved to the assisted living facility, many of their needs were met. My father couldn't keep up with the care Mom needed and the staff was very dependable and grew to really care about both of my parents. They even loved Nellie, the Terrorist, and always wanted to take care of her when my dad was gone. But living in a more communal situation presented another health risk. When one resident had the flu, it could spread so quickly that quarantine was sometimes the only alternative. Most of the time, the facility acted quickly and just the ill resident was impacted. But one particularly bad strain of flu left the entire building in a lock-down mode for almost a week.

While mail and phone solicitation isn't necessarily fraud, it gradually became clear to me that the volume of mail and phone contact was becoming an issue with my elderly father. It wasn't an issue for *him*; in fact, he opened every piece of mail and talked with every telemarketer. And that was the issue with me-he actually thought they cared about him and his well-being. And he was beginning to buy things and empty promises. My father was lonely after Mom died and his days were long. I think his love of mail-call goes back to his military days and it was also a welcome break in the routine of his day. His generation is not as suspecting and cynical, which is exactly what companies that prey on the elderly know. Letters addressed to my dad looked very personal and because so much information is easily obtained today, the letters even spoke to his personal interests.

The promises were endless:

Military honors and medals he qualified for

Eternal health

Prizes just for returning a card

Money is waiting in your name! Just sign and return this postage-free card!

Sexual prowess (yes-even the elderly are targeted)

When my father was no longer able to live in the assisted living facility and we moved him to an adult family home, his mail was forwarded to me. I was amazed at the number of solicitations that found their way to my mailbox addressed to my dad. Now, I'll start all over opting him out at my address. I battled with telemarketers and even credit card companies to have charges reversed, the result of his "accidentally" checking or not checking certain boxes. The credit card companies required a Durable Power of Attorney. In fact, that single document is so important that I made multiple copies and used most of them when my dad could no longer handle his affairs. That is one of the things that I did right in the process of helping my parents on their final path.

Now…if I could just get rid of all of the mail…

Tips for Safety Issues and the Elderly

Dawna says

1. A life alert button is an extremely helpful and economical investment for a parent that lives at home.

2. Review safety issues somewhat frequently. Scams against seniors unfortunately change quickly.

3. Chastising parents over a slip up on a safety issue, just keeps them from communicating with you honestly in the future. Who wants to feel stupid?

Marky says

1. Mail fraud directed at senior citizens is a growing concern. There are some steps you can take to slow the onslaught of mail and telemarketing calls.

2. Educate your parent. You can find information about a burgeoning industry that preys on the elderly. Go to www.USBoomers.com to educate yourself and your parent. The information underlines the importance of paying close attention to the mail and calls your elderly parent is receiving.

3. The Federal Trade Commission allows you some control in opting out of mail. The site is very easy to follow and allows you to permanently stop many solicitations.

4. Calling 1-888-382-1222 from your parent's phone allows you to opt out of many telemarketing calls to their number.

5. The National Council for the Prevention of Crime is also an educational site that offers support for Baby Boomers and others caring for our elderly population.

Chapter Six

PETS

STINKY BINKY

Dawna writes

The cat saga began quite accidentally after I had already left home. I have a brother thirteen years younger than I, who went to put some trash in the garbage can outside one day and found the family's first cat. He was one of those Morris looking cats, all orange with quite full fur. Daryl named him Fuzzy and we were off into a cat era that lasted about three and a half decades.

I'm a dog person myself. The appeal of cats eludes me. Most of them don't come running to greet you when you arrive home. They don't wag their tails and bounce around to make you feel validated and adored. I guess I need unconditional love displayed more than cat lovers. That's embarrassing to admit.

As cats go, Fuzzy was inoffensive and had some limited charms. My brother and mother adored him. Fuzzy did, however, occasionally escape the house and get into some skirmishes which ran up some vet bills. Mom is constitutionally opposed to bills. So it was Fuzzy to whom we must credit the five words most uttered by my mother. These words should appear on my mom's grave marker. The five words we will always associate with our mother are

DON'T LET THE CAT OUT!

Any time anyone entered or left the house Mom said

Don't let the cat out.

In the summertime with a pool filled with grandchildren in the backyard and the bathroom inside, you could hear this command one hundred times in an afternoon.

After Fuzzy came Sam. Sam was a pit bull in a cat suit. That cat was absolutely terrifying. He would hiss at us each time we entered Mom's house. He didn't just hiss, he would stalk toward you like a lion as he hissed. He would arch his back, point his tail skyward, bare his teeth, hiss and reflect your death back to you in his furrowed eyes. Sam was deceptively beautiful, white with a few nicely placed black patches, but I'm certain his parents lived in the Cincinnati Zoo. The only one Sam feared was Mom. Whenever he displayed his real personality Mom would smack him on the snout. He'd cuddle up to her and apologize. Then he'd plan his next assault on Mom's offspring. When we told her how Sam treated us, she'd accuse us of exaggeration. Sam would sit on her lap docilely and smirk in our direction as she petted him.

But the real cat of Mom's lifetime was Binky. Binky was given to Mom by my brother and his wife before Sam died. I think they thought Binky might tame Sam and also help keep Mom company when Sam passed away. My mom allowed my daughter Kelsey to name the new cat because Kelsey was five years old and battling cancer at the time. There was no way Kelsey could have looked eighteen years into the future and realize how incontinent Binky would become. It was just sheer luck that she chose a name that rhymed so well with stinky.

It was unfortunate that Binky arrived during Sam's final years, because she did pick up some of Sam's ways. To the rest of us she could be threatening on a bad day, and aloof on a good day. Again her charms were saved for Mother. But was she ever a companion and a comfort to my mother! She was a beautiful calico cat who was my mom's closest companion for eighteen years. They had their routines and Mom would describe them to me by phone in great detail whether I was interested or not.

Each time Mom was hospitalized great elaborate plans were made for Binky. My niece Missi, an animal lover, dog groomer and vet's assistant would move into Mom's house to give Binky daily care spelled out in detail by Mom. Eventually when Binky was in his mid-teens he became incontinent.

Mom's house began to smell worse and worse. The carpets were stained and the stench was close to unbearable. This was especially hard on my daughter, Jodi, who has a full blown cat allergy. Even sitting in the car with Mother who was wearing clothing from Binkyland would trigger Jodi's allergies. Before long it was an effort just to go and visit Mom or pick her up to take her places, because of the overwhelming smell. Binky's kidneys began to fail. Mom was so distraught that my niece came weekly to Mom's home and injected fluids into the cat to keep her alive for two more years or so.

It sounds insane but none of us could picture Mom surviving long without that cat. Binky at eighteen years old was a bag of bones with an emanating stench, but she didn't cry from discomfort. I honestly try not to force Mom on issues. Especially in the case of an adored pet, I think the owners who most love them have to make the call in life and death situations. Mom went in for a hospitalization and we each assumed our roles in keeping both Mom and Binky alive. This was complicated by an unexpected elongated stay for Mom due to complications following surgery. But Mom eventually recovered and was in the nursing home soon to go home. For weeks we had been feeding Binky, injecting fluids, giving pills, cleaning stains, changing litter and trying to be a companion to Binky scared crazy that the cat would die before Mom could come home.

I had even bigger worries. The nursing home assigned a social worker to visit Mom's home before she was released. I knew when they smelled the stench in Mom's house they would claim the place was unfit for human inhabitants. I was mortified. Cleaning the carpets wouldn't help. We had tried that many times. Was I going to be the first daughter to be proclaimed an unfit daughter? Could they take my mom away and make her go to a home? I was honestly worried and embarrassed about this.

Mom looked at me from her bed in the nursing home and said a sentence I couldn't believe. We hadn't been talking about anything in particular. She said

Daun, I think it is time to let Binky go, don't you?

I was shocked but agreed calmly. She had obviously been thinking about this. She asked me to get Missi to take Binky to the vet and have her put to sleep. (When I told Missi this she almost asked for a signed affidavit, she was so stunned about Grandma's change of heart.) Mom went on to say she wanted Binky cremated. Mom wants Binky's ashes in her own coffin when she dies. This is another wish I will honor. As Mom's loyal companion, Binky has served our whole family well.

The social worker did allow Mom back into her home, but put her in touch with the county senior services. They came to Mom's house and asked Mom what kinds of services she needed to stay in her home. Mom admitted that she had a little trouble keeping her home clean. As the social worker was sitting in Mom's living room surrounded by the aroma of now dead Binky's kidney failure when this conversation took place, the social worker suggested the county office replace her carpet. What kind of a miracle was this? The best kind. Mom had worked hard all her life. She had never asked anyone for a nickel. None of us could believe this wonderful turn of events. We thought it was some kind of misunderstanding on Mom's part. But it happened.

Binky's stench is gone. We can now enjoy visiting our mother again. We are more grateful than I can put into words. It was a new day for Mom and all of us. I was amazed again about what good things can happen when you don't force someone into an uncomfortable decision. Mom has a way of knowing what is right for her. Don't we all? In my view Mom has earned the right to make important decisions in her own time frame. When I am patient and allow her the time to work through her decisions, I continue to learn important lessons from her. Mom recovered and even thrived after the loss of Binky. But she alone created the time table.

Nellie, the Terrorist

Marky writes

Most of my childhood memories include pets. Our youngest daughter inherited her grandmother's unconditional love of pets. Today, she rescues greyhounds and when she was 16, she raised a puppy for Canine Companions for Independence. Jasper found his "calling" as he worked with his owner, an occupational therapist. He would visit elderly patients who needed therapy, always able to nudge a smile from patients as they remembered their own dogs from earlier times. I have just finished organizing the pictures of my 40 year marriage. The many photos of pets peeking at the camera are tangible proof of their everlasting companionship, forever weaving through our lives.

My mother's love for pets was surpassed only by her unconditional love for me-and, okay, for my brothers, too. Mom told me stories of her cat, Aloysious, the Depression Cat. Mom would dress that cat up in doll clothes and push her around in her doll buggy. I still have that doll buggy and through the years, I have often found one of my cats sleeping in it.

When my mother had what was to be the first of many debilitating strokes, she talked me into going to the Humane Society with her to pick out a kitty. My father was enjoying the lack of vet bills, vacation care, etc. that they were experiencing for the first time in their 55 year marriage. But Mom won that battle and off we went. She named the little black kitten Nellie. Cute.

This cat was a terror.

She chewed the leather trim off of a brand new pair of my shoes, ate anything made of Styrofoam, and one time, dragged an entire frozen chicken from the kitchen to the family room. Mom had not yet read the articles about only thawing things in the refrigerator. They found the thawed chicken a day later, behind the couch. The benefits of this cat were not apparent to me, but Mom loved her.

When another stroke left Mom in a rehabilitation facility for a few months, Nellie's loyalty was tested. She moved her allegiance to my dad. I added this to my list of reasons for not liking Nellie. But later, she proved her worth when my mother was gone, leaving my dad alone after 65 years of marriage.

During the year my dad was still able to live in the assisted living facility after Mom was gone, I would bring him out to my house for weekends. He didn't want to leave Nellie, so I would pack her up and bring her too. By that time we had developed a mutual dislike for each other. She gave me no points for my part in rescuing her from the Humane Society or for making sure my dad never ran out of the best cat food or for cleaning her litter when my dad forgot. I also had to replace the foam on several walkers and wheelchairs, because she had eaten it.

Taking her to the vet naturally fell on me. Once, I put her kennel on the SMALL hill next to my car to unload some things and her kennel accidentally (I promise) rolled down the LITTLE hill. I truly felt bad. I took her into the apartment, releasing her from the cat carrier.

What's wrong with Nellie? She seems upset, Mom observed.

Nothing Mom. You know she doesn't like me and I took her to the vet for shots.

Mom didn't say anything, but, like all Moms, she knew there was more to the story. Nellie and I just glared at each other.

In spite of lugging 25 lb. containers of cat litter, cleaning it when my dad forgot, replacing numerous arms on Mom's wheelchair that Nellie had eaten, vacuuming millions of pieces of chewed Styrofoam from the carpet, caring for her at my house when my dad was able to travel after Mom died, the cat did have some worth. She knew what her job in life was and she took it very seriously. She was a high-maintenance piece of work while Mom was alive. And Mom loved her. When my dad was alone, Nellie sat on his lap every single evening for over a year while he was still able to live in the assisted living facility. And she liked football and the History Channel. She over-looked marginally clean cat litter and for some reason I could never figure out, all of the caregivers loved her. I will be forever grateful to my brother for taking her when my dad needed to leave the facility.

And I will give her credit. She kept my parents company through the darkest time of their lives. I was there, but I was a whirlwind of activity, needs and must-dos. Nellie just sat on their laps.

Tips for Pets and Elderly Parents

Dawna says

1. Like it or not, loving your parents means honoring their pet.

2. Enlist family members to help. Surely there is a pet lover somewhere in the family. While I was at Mom's side in the hospital my niece took over most of the pet care, though all of us had to help. One purchased food and litter. One fed and watered and changed the litter box.

3. Even more than most other issues, I think giving your parent the judgment call on important decisions about their pets, is a necessity. Strong attachments can't be rationalized away.

4. When my mom was in the nursing home, my niece's dog (who was trained as a therapy dog) was always welcomed. These visits helped Mom and the other residents. Some seniors relate to animals better than other humans.

Marky says

1. I found that my parents' cat was very important to them in so many ways. They felt needed as they cared for her. Nellie the Terrorist added so much warmth and companionship to their days. Since pets have always been a part of their lives, it was important that they were able to continue enjoying a pet, even if she was a terror.

2. Many studies have proven the value of pets as companions for the elderly; the list of benefits includes

   a. Exercise

   b. Stress relief

   c. Unconditional love and companionship

   d. Caring for a pet makes the person feel needed

   e. Most assisted living and rehabilitation facilities allow pets because they realize the value to their residents when pets are included.

Chapter Seven

DOCTOR VISITS

A ROCKET TO HEAVEN THROUGH THE DOCTOR'S OFFICE

Dawna writes

My elderly mother loves to visit her doctor. I don't blame her. He is a caring man, a great listener well beyond the norm in his profession. I love to see the way he interacts with my mother. He has the right mix of empathy, humor, and concern and that warms my heart and reassures me.

However, I don't enjoy those doctor's visit as much as my mom. Why? I am her transportation *and* her target. Maneuvering to his office has become more challenging. Getting Mom in and out of the car is an increasing stress. His examining room is too far away from the lobby for my mother's walking and breathing capabilities. Mom has to sit on her walker and take a couple of rests on her way to his room. Each time she has to stop she is frustrated. When she is frustrated she turns her annoyance my way. There's a hotline number for children who are victims of child abuse when we are little, but no such number for an adult caring for a parent.

She is convinced her doctor can "fix" her. She wants him to take her pain away. She wants him to give her maneuverability back to her. She wants to feel and navigate like a fifty-year old woman, not an eighty-eight year old great grandma. She looks upon these visits as a social event and will constantly say to him

There is one more thing I wanted to ask you about. Oh what was it?

This is after she has exhausted her long written list. She enjoys keeping his attention on her. She enjoys keeping *everyone's* attention on her. I, however, am aware of his patient load and embarrassed about the way she demands his extended time.

This week we were facing another one of those doctor visits. I felt my tension rising. I decided to try and explain to Mom about some of my frustrations. I hoped to "prep" her a little. I calmly told her about some of the things she said to me on our last visit to his office. A lady I had never met heard my mom talking to me in the lobby and was shocked at her rudeness and irritability directed toward me. This lady actually came up to me and patted me on the shoulder gave me her sympathy and wished me luck.

> *Good luck, honey. You are going to need it!*

She actually said those words as she patted me on the shoulder.

I replied

> *I'm going straight to heaven when my time comes, you know?*

Her reply?

> *On a rocket!*

I shared that story with Mom. At first she claimed it couldn't be true. But I supplied too many details about what Mom had said to me for her to deny the story completely. She looked a little sheepish for a bit.

I also addressed the way she ties up the doctor's time.

> *Mom, have you noticed those little signs in the hair salon that say, 'I'm a beautician, not...'*

> *...a magician.* She finished my thought and laughed a little.

I continued

> *Exactly. I think you believe your doctor is Jesus, but he isn't. He's a doctor, not Jesus. However much he wants to help, you are eighty-eight, not fifty. Even I am sixty-four and don't feel like I'm fifty. He has tried every arthritis medicine*

known to man. He can't make you feel thirty years younger than you are no matter how long you talk to him.

She answered.

I know.

And in that moment she *does* know. But it isn't long until she is talking about going back to the doctor again so that he can make her feel better.

I pray a great deal when I am with my mom. I pray before I get out of my car in her driveway. I pray when I see her number on caller ID before I pick up the phone. I pray for patience so one day I can look back and be proud of the way I treated her through these challenging years. Is there a pill for patience? I try and rerun all the good times we've had over the years like a video loop in my head. But, I'll be honest, some days I pray for that hotline for sixty year old children who are being verbally abused by their parents. Is there a doctor who can fix that? I hope so.

But, to be honest, those doctor visits could be so much worse. We are fortunate that Mom's doctor is perfect for her. He is a wonderful combination of caring and humor. He is a soft spoken man who is very active in his church and revered in the community. As Mom has aged, her language and humor have become quite bawdy. Thank goodness he "gets" her humor. Here is an exact dialogue of portions of our latest doctor's visit.

Mom (to her male doctor)

Doctor, I'm telling you my hand hurts. I can't write well anymore. I can't unscrew a jar. I'm having trouble dressing

> *myself. Tell me, how would <u>you</u> like it if <u>you</u> couldn't put <u>your</u> bra on in the morning?*

Doctor

> *Well, I think what I do in private is nobody's business.*

The man may not be Jesus but he *is* a saint AND a comic genius. I swear he didn't laugh, didn't even grin or give me a sidelong look. I think he avoided my eyes because he knew I'd be embarrassed about all this bra talk in mixed company. He just delivered that line with a straight face. Mom's hearing is so bad it went right over her head. I worked hard not to fall on the floor laughing. I have laughed out loud about that one line a dozen times since.

And then later in the same visit…

Mom

> *Doctor, I'm just not ambitious. Is that the right word, Dauna?*

Dauna (me)

> *Yeah Mom, that's the right word. I might have said 'lazy' but you're sitting too close to me and I was afraid you might hit me.*

Mom

> *Oh shut up. But I guess that's the truth, doctor. I just don't want to do anything. I don't want to clean. I don't want to exercise. I just sit around like a blob, watch television, and do nothing. I just don't feel like getting off my chair.*

Doctor

Well Virginia, I really don't have a pill for laziness. But if you really don't want to do anything at all, we can find you a nice nursing home and they can do <u>everything</u> for you.

Mom

Go to hell!

That time he grinned.

THE DOCTOR AND MY DAD'S CAR KEYS

Marky writes

The concern started slowly, as absolutely everything about my parents' aging. *Knowing* what is logical and *living* that logic are often very much at odds. Looking back on my mother's first stroke, I do remember people saying things like *You should move them closer to you* and *It will only get worse.* I resented the obvious truth of those statements. Early in the process, when my mother's stroke changed who she was in so many ways, I started a notebook to record what each doctor, social worker and therapist said, along with their phone numbers. That was one of the smartest things I did. There were days when the only tangible resource in my life was that book. I also conferenced with an eldercare specialist, the one who termed the phrase "aging deliberately" in her Seattle newspaper column. Her advice?

Move your parents closer

My husband and I were able to convince them to move to an assisted living facility about 25 miles from us and close to our married daughters. For the first 3 years, the caregivers took care of Mom's needs, I took care of everything in between and my father was able to drive Mom to doctor appointments and out to my house in the accessible van. I look back on the years of being the primary go-to adult child caregiver and even though my parents weren't in my home, I lived with a sense of impending crisis.

I developed the ridiculous habit of crossing my fingers whenever the phone rang, reverting to childhood tactics to ward off evil. Most phone calls were normal, but many were not: mom fell out of her wheelchair and broke her leg, my dad passed out several different times, the cat ate all of the foam off of Mom's wheelchair arms, the wheelchair didn't work, and both of my parents had strokes, leading to stays in nursing homes. I drove home exhausted many nights. We soldiered on even as I saw the look of regret in my parents' eyes. They knew how much they needed me and their gratefulness was marred by the deep fear of advancing age.

The first time my father passed out, he was in the dining room and help appeared quickly. But this was to accelerate my slowly developing paranoia of his driving. Mom was no longer able to intuit life as she always had. My mother was the kind who lavished unconditional love. She made me believe I was amazing. She had many friends and as I became more a part of the visits of their long-time friends, I learned how loved my mother really was. But she was different now and I grieved that loss. But the busyness of life and the need to put out as many of the fires as I could took precedence over giving way to feelings.

Slowly, my father's driving became a consuming issue. I started with an amiable discussion. Mom had a faraway look in her eyes and my dad's agreement was outwardly sincere, but I knew even then that he had no intention of giving up his keys. I became subversive. I would call the doctor's office before appointments, speak to the nurse and ask her to warn the doctor. I would accost his doctor in the hallway during an office visit to warn him ahead of time.

Then my father had another episode of passing out and as I sat next to his bed in the hospital I noticed the young Korean female hospitalist walk in the room. Since my chair was out of my dad's vision, I mimicked having hands on a steering wheel to her. She got it. My father is a Korean War Veteran and a product of an earlier paternalistic society. But I watched with tears in my eyes as she took his hands and said,

> *Mr. Mathews, I know you will honor my direction that you not drive anymore.*

I held my breath. And my dad answered,

> *For you, I will stop driving.*

I slowly reveled in the feeling of a solved problem. And I looked forward to taking care of my 88 year old father. The reverie was not to last.

We were to lose my mother to a stroke not long after that. Coping with that loss, moving to a smaller apartment and even taking a few trips kept my dad thoughtful and accepting about driving…for a while. Even though I spent Wednesdays with him, taking him to appointments, shopping and lunch, there came a day where I felt the battle brewing again. The episodes of passing out remained undiagnosed and had not re-occurred for long enough that, in my dad's mind, he was cured. He seemed to overlook the fact that he had also had a stroke.

Indeed the battle resumed. I enlisted the help of my dad's doctor, a geriatric specialist with whom my dad and I had built a relationship during the past 4 years. Through a break-down in communication or the tenacity of my dad (I was never able to determine exactly what happened) the doctor seemed to be on my dad's side. When I was finally able to connect with him, this was our conversation:

The doctor

> *I can't in good conscience interfere with your father's personal rights.*

My response

> *Where in your medical training does it say that seniors who have a compromising physical condition have the right to increase risk to others who are driving? You have made this situation infinitely more difficult for my family and me.*

After the discussion with my dad's doctor, the battle took on a life of its own. My dad's standard answer to any discussion was *I flew B-26 airplanes over 1600 hours and you want to take my keys away.* The fact that he had been in his 20s then and was 87 at this point did not seem to register with him. I admit that I ranted at my father more than once. I tried every argument until I finally threw the keys on the floor, left and called my daughter to pick me up. Naturally, she was on my side, with the pure, black and white passion of the young. But it was an empty victory. The good relationship with my father was badly shaken. I just could not forgive him for what I perceived as a lack of gracious acceptance of aging.

About this time, my father flew to Arizona to see my uncle and called me halfway through his visit to say that he would give the keys and the car back as soon as he returned home. I had called my uncle to warn him of the driving issue, and although I know my uncle talked with him, I was never to learn the real reason he finally agreed to give up his keys. But I will always suspect that he had a scare while driving to the VA for an appointment on a very rainy day just prior to his trip.

My father was to suffer a debilitating stroke not long after he returned from that trip. Looking back, I can say that the issue would have taken care of itself, possibly with no harm to anyone. But I believe that I did what I knew was right. And that, in this one area, my father's need to hold on to his past will stand out in my mind as one of the most difficult times of the 7 years I cared for my parents. The concern and time spent on this battle should not have happened. I can't change that now, but there is this value: I will be gracious and honor my children when they tell me it is time.

Another year has gone by. My father lives with dementia now and tells me he *flew 12 missions last night* at least once a week. The pain of the driving issue has dimmed, of course. The powerful bond of familial love, tested with sleepless nights when our children are babies, the turmoil of teenagers and the natural child-becoming-parent time, turns out to be one of life's deepest, most everlasting and rewarding necessities.

TIPS FOR DOCTOR VISITS

Dawna says

1. I let mom and her doctor run their visits. I interject my thoughts only when I think they might shed some light. Example: When she complained about her hand, I mentioned to him that she says it always feels cold, but when you touch her hand it feels warm. He said, "That tells me her circulation is good. It is probably a nerve problem." If she had told him about the coldness, I wouldn't have said anything.

2. I had to ask to speak to an office manager at the doctor's office because her prescriptions were being sent to the wrong pharmacy about one out of every six times. That finally solved the problem.

3. I found I needed lots of patience on the days of doctors' visits. If I made a pact with myself that I was going to be more patient than anyone could possibly expect, the days went better.

4. Both my mom and I are very satisfied with her general practitioner doctor. This is the best scenario.

5. Occasionally I have been less satisfied with one of her specialists. I allow her to choose her physicians, but the doctor then must hear my concerns. I look out for her best interests. We are a package deal.

Marky says

1. Making a list of questions ahead of time will make the best use of the doctor's time.

2. Even if you are able to attend appointments with your parent, understanding all of their medical issues is a challenge.

3. Visit www.icareinsite.com and learn about a dependable service that will obtain all of your parent's medical records and translate them for you. Imagine understanding all of their medications!

4. I also tried to stay in the background so that my parents could maintain more control and self-respect. I only added essential information. With situations that require more careful handling, such as driving, it can be very helpful to call and talk with the doctor ahead of time. Although this wasn't helpful in my situation, it has been beneficial for friends.

5. Awareness is bringing change. The Insurance Institute for Highway Safety recently completed a study, finding that many older drivers are monitoring any personal impairment and making adjustments. With safer cars and driving classes for older drivers, we are beginning to address the issue.

Dauna's Family Album

Dauna's Mom, Age 4; How Dauna played outside before moving to the suburbs; Dauna's Mom: Graduation Day 1941; Wanted: A man who made eggs fall on the floor.; Mom & my elbow doing a bathing beauty pose.

Dauna'a Parents; NOT Ozzie and Harriet; Dauna blowing out birthday candles about the age of 'The Talk.'; Dauna's 5 grandchildren; Grandma, Dauna, & Kelsey in Washington DC. Tiny white dots are all flames of candles of children with cancer.; Kelsey 1982-1999, she loved her robe days. We loved her.

Marky's Family Album

The Skiing Princess; The Boat (Marilyn Monroe in the background); The Sandwich of Four Generations; Marky and office partner Marion; Marky's brothers Gary (L) and Bart (R) -50th Anniversary; Craig and Betty 1944

Betty and Craig with Nellie the Terrorist, 2007; Three generations – Craig, Ashley and Anna, 2011; Betty and Craig revisiting Oregon State in 1998; Oregon State Game October 2010; Marky's grandchildren; Betty and Gary 1946; Craig's cockpit and his ever-present picture of Betty

Chapter Eight

ADVOCACY

LISTEN TO YOUR MOTHER

Dawna writes

Listen to your mother.

I wonder how many times we heard that sentence while we were growing up? My mom molded those words into my psyche. My dad echoed them. As a grandparent myself, I remind my grandchildren to listen to their mother (my own daughter).

But as our parents age the task becomes a little harder and sometimes we completely fail. These days I know that my mom wants me to call her every day, but for her to feel "heard" those calls can often last an hour or more. Also sometimes my mom, in her late eighties has some trouble relating to what is going on in my world. Phone calls are generally one sided including predominantly the same stories she has told me before. No, she doesn't have Alzheimer's. It's just that she doesn't drive anymore and her world has become smaller and more repetitive. She has no new news to report, but she still needs my ears.

About a decade ago Mom felt so badly that she asked me to take her to the hospital emergency room. She was complaining of a funny feeling in her arms, and just an ache-all-over sensation. Typically that would mean a trip to the doctor, but I could tell she felt awful and that she was afraid she was dying. An ache in her arms? She had never complained of that before. Was it a heart attack? So off to the emergency room we went. After many tests that strange sensation in her arms proved to be a urinary tract infection. Go figure. Only one night in the hospital being hydrated and pumped full of antibiotics and she was able to go home.

Several years later she experienced a big setback following a knee surgery. By this age (early eighties) mom was not tolerating anesthetics or pain medications very well. By her eighties Mom's surgeries were nightmare experiences for me. In fact I had been opposed to the knee surgery altogether because of her frightening reaction to anesthetics during her previous hip surgery. I refused to go to the orthopedic surgeon for a consultation with Mom. But the two of them (Dr. and grandma) plotted together and scheduled a second appointment that Mom begged me to attend.

When the doctor was in the examining room he showed me Mom's knee x-rays. I glanced at the film and recounted to him all the things that had gone awry during her previous hip surgery. I visited the hospital on my lunch hour the day after her hip operation and found her with only her shoulders on the hospital bed. Her oxygen level was in the 60's when I arrived. She was receiving a morphine drip that I was unaware of and was not at all cognizant of her surroundings. She couldn't even understand to push the button to summon a nurse.

Over and over she tried to get out of bed. No amount of reasoning could stop her. The catheter she was wearing gave her the sensation that she had to go to the bathroom. She couldn't understand that the catheter would take care of the urine. Morphine was in control and Mother "wasn't home."

The morphine was also repressing her respiration and she had to continue to use oxygen. None of this was explained to me. We had never experienced this after surgery before. Again and again she took out her oxygen tubes because in her altered state she just kept thinking she had to blow her nose. I not only had to spend the night right next to her in the hospital, I had to stay *awake* and vigilant to keep her in the bed and uninjured for her three remaining days in the hospital.

As I explained this to the doctor he said,

> *I was her surgeon. I wonder why I never knew any of this?*

I told him why he was unaware. It was because he never came in the room once during the three days that I stayed next to Mom. Oh, it would be marked on the chart that a doctor (hospitalist) had visited. But I never once left that room, not for a drink or a bathroom break. I used Mom's bathroom. And no matter how many times I asked the nurses to see him, or another doctor, none appeared.

But then, back in the examining room about the knee, he delivered the clincher phrase.

Do you want your mom to live in pain?

Mom's sad and pleading face accompanied the doctor's plea, but I still replied with my concern.

I want my mom to live.

How do you "listen to your mother" and stand firm when the doctor is accusing you of dooming her to a life of pain? The surgery was scheduled against my better judgment, because Mom always believes the doctors can make her feel better. She *wants* them to make her feel better. The surgery was scheduled also at the most inconvenient time possible for me. It was the Friday before Labor Day and I was a teacher.

The recovery from this ensuing surgery was far, far worse. They didn't use morphine but following surgery gave her a drug that caused mom to hallucinate to the point that she was screaming for the police at the top of her lungs. The hospital called me at about 11:00 pm and asked me to return to the hospital. They had to move patients to other areas of the hospital because of Mom's shrieking. Once again I had to stay at Mom's side 24/7 until she was sent to a nursing facility for rehabilitation.

That stay in the rehabilitation center lasted two days until she was returned to the hospital via ambulance. The emergency situation by this point was pandemonium. Mom's bowels and intestines had shut down. A tube was inserted down her nose to release the poison collecting in her abdomen while the emergency room doctors kept asking me for the name of a surgeon. Every instinct in me knew Mom would not survive another surgery. However, only hours later at 4 am the hospital staff said if I would not provide the name of a surgeon, they would assign one. Clearly they believed surgery was imminent and the only answer.

At 4 am I called a good friend who is a former nurse. She was vacationing with another group of women in Minneapolis at the Mall of America! Imagine my reluctance to wake her in the middle of the night, but I was desperate. I asked her if she knew of a surgeon who wasn't quick to operate. I apologized for calling her in the middle of the night but explained my circumstances. Within half an hour she called me back with a name she had procured from her current nurse friends whom she had phoned and awakened back home in Cincinnati.

He was exactly the right man for the situation (thank you to my nurse friends). He was a surgeon who listened to family members. He was a surgeon who visited Mom's room twice a day. He was a surgeon who believed with me that in Mom's situation surgery was a last resort.

It took another eight long days to solve the puzzle. Eight days when my mom wasn't herself at all. Eight more days of my being at her bedside in the hospital 24/7. Again she couldn't even understand how to call a nurse. She was so "out of it" that one day while I was eating a chicken salad sandwich, a nurse gave me a handout on dementia. She thought she was helping me understand Mom's situation. Did she think I was an out of town family member who was disconnected from Mom's reality? Who knows? Mom wasn't senile then or even now, a half dozen years later. She still lives independently in her own home and handles all her own bills among other tasks. She does now, however, rely on family members for transportation and other chores she finds difficult to do on her own.

One night at 2 am about eight days into that long scary hospital stay, Mom woke up having a lucid moment. She turned to me and said,

> *Daun, Do you remember the time you brought me to the hospital and I had that funny sensation in my arms? That's how I feel now. What was wrong with me then?*

It only lasted for less than a minute. Then she slid back into her delirium. The next morning I asked the nurse to do a urinalysis. The nurse was skeptical.

> *She couldn't possibly have a urinary infection. She is on too many antibiotics.*

I stood my ground.

> *Humor me.*

I didn't want to tell her Mom had "that sensation in her arms." She would think I was crazy. Maybe I was crazy, but I decided I had to listen to my mother.

Later that day the surgeon stopped by and asked

> *Who ordered the urinalysis?*

I apologized and admitted I was the culprit. I told him not to blame the nurse; she had warned me it would show nothing. He then explained

Your mom has a raging urinary infection. How did you suspect that? And did you know that a urinary infection can shut down the bowels? We have probably just found the solution to her problem.

I was stunned.

No, I knew none of that. I'm not a nurse.

But then I explained to him what my mom had told me in the middle of the night. In two days Mom was back to herself and out of the hospital. I'm so grateful that I was at her side at 2 am at just that one lucid moment and remembered to "listen to my mother".

In hindsight, this story scares me even more than when I was living it. In medical school I'm certain there is a class that warns future doctors to "listen to the patient" and/or hopefully "listen to the family of the patient". I'm grateful to the med students who didn't skip class on that day and took the advice to heart. But still it takes my breath away at how important it was for me to be there in the middle of the night and to listen to my mother and then act on what she said. I even had to stand firm and with confidence when I made my request. In many days of trying to problem solve only my mother gave us that one opportunity to figure it out.

What about her knee? The surgery never improved her mobility or stopped her pain. But I must share that I did enjoy calling the knee surgeon into the hospital on a Sunday and showing him how Mom's condition had deteriorated following his surgery. I also told him never again to ask me in front of my mother,

Do you want your mother to live in pain?

My reply would be the same.

I want my mother to live.

Only this time I would stand my ground with more confidence. Sometimes for a courteous person it is quite difficult to stand up to medical personnel. But if we don't advocate for our loved ones, who will?

It Wasn't About 'The Right to Die... It Was About My Mother

Marky writes

My mother died at 8:20 on a Saturday morning after 10 days in a hospice center. It wasn't in her home and she wasn't surrounded by the three generations of family members, including a husband of 65 years. I had been there every day for at least a few hours. I wasn't there the morning she left us. But I am absolutely, positively okay with that and I am certain my mother was too.

On January 15, 2010, my mother had what was to be her last stroke. Earlier strokes had left her first with a walker and then in a wheelchair. She and my father spent 5 years in an assisted living facility because being wheelchair bound is a challenge, especially for an elderly person. My brothers and my husband

and I convinced them to move to a facility closer to us, a blessing that was to be constantly reinforced.

Arriving at the hospital emergency room that day, and hearing the ER doctor's prognosis, I realized we were probably walking a final path with Mom. The family gathered. Mom did survive the first crucial 24 hours, and was moved to intensive care by Sunday. That's when the questions, concerns and sleepless nights began. Living in a "right to die" state takes on a new meaning when one's mother is involved. There are no rules. No matter what I knew about my mother's wishes, no matter what state law says and no matter what doctors predict in terms of rehabilitation, we were on our own. I will be eternally grateful that my mother had made her wishes known and that we had it in writing. And she had always told me she did not want to be in a bed at the end of her life. Those important facts were our guidelines. The heart, though, searches for something more. My elderly father was naturally distraught but did not want his love of 65 years to linger with no hope of recovery. My brother was clear in his support of Mom's wishes. I knew the path we needed to follow, but still… it was lonely. It was lonely because no one asked if the feeding tube should be inserted. It was just done. And there was my mother, living exactly the way she did not want to live. The hospitalization doctor was nice…but there was no eye contact when she made the statement

> *With extensive rehabilitation, your mother might regain some strength.*

I began to panic until I remembered the ER doctor. His credibility was what I needed. There was to be a shift change shortly and I wanted to talk with him before I met the new hospitalist.

I headed to emergency, hoping he was on duty. He was. Miraculously, I was talking with him within 10 minutes. He told me that doctors are trained to save lives until we tell them otherwise and that I needed to trust and honor my mother's wishes. Laws concerning an individual's right to die have a place in our society, but they mean nothing if you don't know what your loved one's wishes are. Such laws are not the protagonist in the play of the final days of one's own mother. I returned to my mother's bedside feeling a profound mixture of confidence and trepidation.

The new hospitalist doctor sat across from my father, looked directly into his eyes and asked him what he was feeling. My father talked of his love for his Betty for 15 minutes. During that time, the doctor said nothing, just listened completely. Then my dad said,

> *Did you notice she has beautiful legs, just like Betty Grable?*
>
> *But she has been so unhappy not being able to use her legs for the last five years. She absolutely would not want to live with even less of her life.*

Even the doctor was crying. Then she said,

> *You're giving your wife the final and greatest gift by honoring her wishes. We will take care of everything and Betty will be completely comfortable.*

I was no longer alone.

Walking into a Hospice Care Center for the first time is a pivotal moment for anyone. You cross the line between 'what if someday' and 'this is it'. I was prepared for feeling lost, scared and disconcerted. Rather, I was oddly comforted. The attention and caring were tangible and palpable. Maybe it was the spacious, comfortable rooms, with family accommodations if they chose to stay...or the harpist...or the flute player...or the art. And here is something else. I had been in several hospitals and care facilities with my parents. The air was different. The smell was different. There was a blending of senses, emotions and reality. Maybe it was the absolute acceptance of each person's path toward death. There was simply no judgment...no expectations-just respect, warmth and caring. A slight furrow on Mom's brow would be cause for discussion of exactly what would bring comfort. The sense of rightness, tinged with warmth, logic and even humor became the rhythm of my days.

The credibility of the nurses was quickly apparent and this I won't forget: Nancy said,

> *Your dad must let your mom know it is okay for her to leave. The dance of long-married couples is their dance and no one else will be able to convey your dad's feelings to your mom.*

She also told me that *hearing is the last sense to go and that Mom would always know when I was there.*

Experience had taught them, though, that patients did not always want family members there. I wondered how I would know. I talked with Mom, although she responded with weakening hand pressure. I read to her: *The Bible,* poetry, her favorite authors and even the book she wrote. Sometimes we just sat and listened to the sound of the water from the small moisture drip that ensured her comfort. I began to learn another way of communication with my mother, a sort of 'feeling between the lines.' Having lost my younger brother several years ago, I was no stranger to the path of grief. But this was different. Each day she changed and I watched my mother die. Where did I find the courage to absorb that reality? I cannot say, but I will always believe that being surrounded by an atmosphere that knows death allowed me to find the grace of acceptance.

On Friday night, after Mom had been at the Hospice Center for 10 days, I told her that I would not come back the next day. Something told me that my ever-independent mother wanted to be alone. My goodbye to my mother followed a heart-comforting harpist who played for my mother alone. I know she heard. I know she felt. She knew she was loved.

I've lived long enough to know what I can absorb and what I should say no to. I asked hospice not to call me if mom were to die in the middle of the night. I am a person who can absorb things much more easily in the light of day, especially in the inherent promise of the morning. On the morning of January 30th, I called, expecting to hear that Mom was gone. She was not. I remember telling my son-in-law that I felt I would have to take my dad back to say good-bye one more time when the phone rang.

Mom was gone.

The time was 8:21. My daughter said,

Baba was independent to the end.

And she reminded me that nearly all of my married life, I had talked with mom every Saturday morning at 8:30.

I didn't hear my mother's voice, but I heard and felt the rightness in my last Saturday morning communication with my mother. All was well.

Tips for Advocating for Your Parent

Dawna says

1. You can be an advocate for your parent in a courteous way. Questioning isn't confrontation unless you make it confrontational.

2. Remember the doctors and nurses have dozens of patients. You can zero in on just one. If she has never received green medicine in her IV before, question if it happens now.

3. *Being uncomfortable now while asking for something a doctor or nurse doesn't believe is necessary, is better than living with regret later after a loved one is gone.*

4. I learned that when my mom is on some pain medications she can become paranoid about life and her caregivers. I had to spend time with her in the medical setting to tell when her complaints were valid or imaginary.

5. Look for the doctors and nurses who will listen. Develop a rapport with them and ask them your questions. It is not always the primary care doctor who will help you the most.

Marky says

1. With time and distance issues, it isn't easy to interview or change doctors. Sometimes, you just have to go with the caregiver or doctor your parent found.

2. The sandwich approach is effective most of the time. When you have an issue, start with a compliment, squeeze in the complaint, and end with a compliment. Then offer a reasonable compromise.

3. However professional the medical staff, no one knows your loved one like you do. Follow your instincts. Speak up on their behalf. If you don't advocate for your loved one, who will?

4. Know your parent's wishes. Don't assume you know. Ask them and listen.

Chapter Nine

NURSING HOMES...
SKILLED NURSING FACILITIES

COOTS AND THE CHRISTMAS GULLS

Marky writes

The great fact in life, the always possible escape from dullness, was the lake. The sun rose out of it, the day began there; it was like an open door that nobody could shut. The land and all its dreariness could never close in on you. You had only to look at the lake, and you knew you would soon be free.
– Willa Cather

Whenever I visit my dad at the Adult Family Home, I enter with some hesitation. I visit 2 or 3 times a week, each visit tempered by his state of mind that day. Dementia has entered the picture, but he always knows me and I'm grateful for that. I'm resentful of the dementia that has robbed my dad of who he was, but I'm also grateful for its numbing power that renders my dad unaware of the life he misses. His thoughts and communication center around my mom, who has been gone for 2 years and his flying days during the Korean War.

> **Your mother was just here and I wish she would stay. She just won't settle down!**
>
> What did she say to you, Daddy?
>
> **We're not going to Hawaii after all.**
>
> Oh.
>
> **I'm really tired today. I was in Tokyo last night and I flew 12 missions.**
>
> I would be tired too! Tell me more about last night.
>
> **I got all of the tomatoes picked up, but did you pick up the ball hoop last night?**

Sometimes, gentle humor works: "I'm glad you got those tomatoes, because that will save me a trip to the store." But not always. When the caregiver calls in the evening, I know my dad is experiencing sundowners, a colloquial term for dementia that worsens in the evening. I try to calm him down on the phone. Sometimes, just hearing my voice is enough. Sometimes the caregiver resorts to a stronger medication dose. I've read all of the articles about over-medicating those in nursing homes and I get the basic human wrongness of controlling the lives of our elderly. But this I also know: I want my dad safe, I respect those who care for him and I want us all to sleep at night. For the most part, a smaller daily dose of an anti-depressant seems to be working.

I thought I had experienced most of the heart-breaking-and-loss-of-independence challenges that aging had in store. I have said good-bye to my mother after sitting next to her bed in the hospice facility for 10 days. We faced a long list of health issues and kept financial concerns at bay. I have finally sorted out most of my parents' possessions. I have grieved, learned and healed. I found that even in the darkest of times, there was caring, love and hope.

But this dementia.

This dementia undermines dignity. And it robs me of a gentle way of accepting my father's failing health. We aren't able to sit together, recalling fond memories. It denies us the comforting rhythm of normal conversation. As I tucked my dad in for his nap, he looked small. He likes the blanket close around him; that cocoon of comfort is one of the few he has left. He looks up at me and says, *Sometimes I forget things*. The simple statement is so deeply profound…and utterly heartbreaking.

I found the Adult Family Home following a stroke that left my dad unable to return to the assisted living apartment, where he had lived for 6 years. The skilled nursing facility determined that he was not progressing and I did not want him to remain there. It was a large and active facility, but the loneliness was palpable, both my father's and my own. At $7000/month, the cost was also unacceptable. At the time, my goals were safety and comfort, proximity and cost. We didn't think my dad would live very long. The adult family home I found could handle my dad's needs, there was room available and the care appeared to be good. The home was modest and certainly not 'state-of-the-art' accessible but I didn't focus on that.

It was the lake.

I focused on the lake. The home sat at the southern end of a beautiful 8 mile long lake not far from my house. As I stood there the first time I walked in, I went back to being a child. I grew up 2 blocks from a lake. I spent hours watching my dad build our first boat. I learned to water ski and became a fairly good slalom skier by the time I was 10.

After we moved him in, I began noticing things that had escaped me before. I worried about his care, his safety, a perceived lack of communication, etc. All of the concerns, fueled by guilt, took a toll on my ability to enjoy visiting my father. I stopped to consider and came up with two solutions. One was that I organized the other adult children. We exchanged emails and we started having once-a-month Dad Desserts when we would all visit at the same time. As we sat by our dads around the table the conversation and laughter of the adult children flowed around the dads. They didn't join in the conversation, but they all knew we were there and they truly enjoyed the normalcy and sense of family.

Another solution was to add recent pictures of each father with a short biography that described their lives, mounted on the wall around the dining table. When visiting caregivers and families of potential residents visited, the dads came alive for them. We adult children centered our conversations around much of what our dads had experienced in their lives. I was able to call Pam, whose father had been there longer than mine and her accepting and sage advice became a source of great comfort to me. The concerns gradually subsided as a sense of home established itself around my dad. And the lake was always there, just a glance away. It was comforting, entertaining and endlessly freeing.

Walking in for our December Dad's Dessert, I looked past the dining room table to see little black bird-ducks congregating near the shore and beautiful "dancing ducks" out in the lake. I stopped and took in the now familiar site of my father in his orange Oregon State sweatshirt, framed by his wheelchair with the lake in the background. That picture is now digitally imprinted on my heart. Bill Jr. explained that the black ducks were coots and that the dancing ducks were just gulls. We settled on Christmas Gulls.

Visiting at lunchtime one day around Christmas, I was the only one sitting at the table with The Dads. The caregiver had stepped out for a minute and I was at the table with 5 gentle souls, each lost in their own dementia and memory-fueled reveries. No one spoke as they ate their lunches. It was true companionable silence. The old hands slowly raised foam-fattened forks for old fingers to grip and cups with lids and double handles. They proudly wore the bibs I had made with airplanes and tractors. The camaraderie was palpable, profound and reflected the wisdom of lives well-spent. Christmas anticipation had mellowed into contentment and each wrinkled face reflected faith. I looked out to the lake and watched the Christmas gulls and the coots. I looked at each dad, sitting beneath pictures of their younger selves. I recognized the deep silence of true faith.

Just gulls and old coots will never be the same to me. The negative connotation has mellowed in my mind to describe men whose lives were worthy, unique, interesting and now full of the sense of experience. The tiny decorated tree and the lights of the holiday danced along with the gulls on the lake; the lake has become an open door that never closes and my dad will soon be free.

THE BAD RAP

Dawna writes

Only once when I was a little girl do I remember going to a nursing home. I was with my grandmother (we called her Mim) who took me along as she visited her sister. I had really never heard anything about Mim's sister. I don't remember much about the visit except that I was asked to talk to the woman in the bed who couldn't speak back to me. She seemed to be living in an older, larger Victorian type home, in an upstairs bedroom. Mostly I remember Mim's sadness.

Many years later I planned several visits taking preschoolers to what we generically called nursing homes to sing to the residents. The seniors loved the little ones. The preschoolers loved those who would make over them, but seemed startled by the residents who couldn't respond or made uncontrolled verbalizations. Every once in a while I would have a parent who wouldn't let their children attend on the days that we went to the nursing home to sing. What was that fear about? I grew up hearing parents and other adults proclaim,

I never want to live in a nursing home!

Yep, it was fear alright. It took me a long time to understand that when people demanded that they never wanted to live in a nursing home that they weren't talking about a place. The two words 'nursing home' were getting a bad rap because of people's own fear of growing older. They were really talking about their fear of facing a time in their lives when they were unable to take care of themselves. They were actually proclaiming

> *I want to live independently without being a burden to anyone. I don't want to live so long that I can't remember my family and friends. I want to die with my dignity intact.*

No, they weren't talking about a place. And in a perfect life, that wish would come true for all of us.

There is a great scene in the movie Grumpy Old Men when Walter Matthau and Jack Lemon, two crusty old guys, walk up to their favorite bait shop on the way to go ice fishing. The door won't open. They eventually realize that their friend, the owner of the shop who was alive yesterday, has died overnight. One of them looks at the other and says,

Lucky S.O.B.

I remember in the movie theater we laughed. I'm not sure I completely understood that scene when I first saw it almost twenty years ago. I was in my forties then. Who wanted to die overnight? But I completely understand that comment now.

Somewhere in the late 1980s (at least in my community) we began to see a big change in what we used to call nursing homes. They were becoming retirement communities, with homes, apartments, beautiful dining rooms, libraries, hair salons and amenities we had never dreamed of having in our senior years. The services they provided were multi-layered. You could live in your own home completely independently on beautifully landscaped grounds, or in an assisted living situation. The seniors became more connected to their communities. Vans full of shopping retirees went on trips and visited the grocery store together.

The first time I was ever in a contemporary style 'nursing home' with my mother, we were going to a craft show. The place was gorgeous, had a gift shop, an ice cream parlor and a beautiful lobby. Of course, it wasn't really a nursing home but a retirement community. But it did have that one wing where most visitors never ventured that provided twenty-four hour nursing care.

My mom has now had three stays in a nursing home. She didn't enter by the front door…the conventional method. No retirement community with a gradual move to assisted living was in the cards for her. She went straight from a fall in her home to a short hospital stay and then off to the dreaded wing of the nursing home. When the doctor announced that necessity every one of us adult kids gasped.

In hindsight we were lucky. Mom chose the same retirement center where we had attended the craft show. Her room was the closest to the end of the hall that entered into the assisted living hallways of apartments, near the physical therapy room. Her stay was just under a month within Medicare guidelines. She still was laying guilt on all of us for her predicament at the time. But she found some wonderful caregivers inside. One of the ladies who worked there exchanged cards and letters and even a visit with Mom in her home after Mom was released.

No, it wasn't Fantasy Island. Mom didn't want to be there. While some caregivers were wonderful, some were just doing their job. (Sounds like the rest of the world.) Mom was required to have a roommate who actually just slept most of the day. Sometimes a resident with dementia would wander in for an unscheduled visit. Mom learned a great deal from the physical therapists, as did all of us. So far Mom has had two more stays in that same wing. She chose to go back there both times. That tells you a great deal about her first visit even though she wasn't sharing enthusiastic compliments during her first stay.

The second time she had a roommate she really enjoyed. Our entire family visited Grandma frequently while she was there. Her children, grandchildren and great grandchildren got a different view of 'the nursing home.' My young teen daughter, Kelsey, even seemed to enjoy it there. She had spent two years of her childhood battling cancer in a hospital bed. She definitely enjoyed *not* being the one in the bed. She enjoyed caring for someone else. Sometimes we would leave her there for a couple of hours with her Grandma. She loved to walk the hallways independently to get something for grandma from the gift shop or ice cream parlor.

Mom spent her whole life dreading a place that was ready to meet her needs when the time came. That was a great lesson for all of us.

It Takes a Village

Marky writes

The Gloaming. We would call it that twilight time of day. Baby boomers enjoy a sort of gloaming time of life when responsibilities have somewhat lessened and your own children are raised, hopefully gainfully employed and you can focus on the wonder of grandchildren. Maybe career responsibilities have lessened and you might be planning to downsize and enjoy friends, family and hobbies.

> *But my gloaming included the increasing needs of my elderly parents.*

I had no idea what this would mean. It isn't that I wasn't willing to help my elderly parents, or that I care only about the well-being of my children and grandchildren. It's that I was woefully unprepared for realities of advanced age: the loss of independence, the concerns over finances, housing and medical needs. One of my longtime favorite poems by Dylan Thomas "Do Not Go Gentle into That Good Night" has now taken on a deeply personal meaning:

> *And you, my father, there on the sad height,*
> *Curse, bless, me now with your fierce tears, I pray.*
> *Do not go gentle into that good night.*
> *Rage, rage against the dying of the light.*

My parents realized they needed to be closer to my husband and me, but they still wanted to live on their own. I'm a planner, organizer and I'm very independent. I figured I could take care of everything-my own busy life and career, and my parents' needs. I gradually learned that everyone needs a Village. You just have to find yours and accept their help.

Your Village might include your siblings, your spouse, your grown children, medical personnel and tireless caregivers and very importantly, grandchildren and even pets. The love of a grandchild for an elderly grandparent tends to be pure and blessedly void of the baggage of many relationships. My grandchildren are accepting, less aware of social conventions and they brought the fresh innocence that was gradually becoming lost to my parents as they entered their final stages of life. My two grandsons loved to see old pictures and happily listened to my dad talk about his flying days. They were especially excited when they were allowed to hold my dad's model airplanes. Beyond my family, I learned as much as I could about my parent's medical situation, developed relationships with their doctors and nurses and I constantly thanked their caregivers.

My mother lived the last 5 years of her life wheelchair-bound, so my grandsons, ages 6 and 4, were used to elderly people, walkers and *don't touch that!* My father continued living in the assisted living facility for over a year after my mother died, enjoying friends and even traveling. Then a stroke left him in a wheelchair and suffering from dementia. He was in a skilled nursing facility for two months. Here is what I did: I quit feeling sorry for myself, for my parent and I accepted the situation. Mercifully, the smells abated-or I just got over them.

> *Instead of walking past residents, I stopped, got down to their wheel chair level...and listened. If you listen around the dementia, past the weakened bodies and into the heart, you'll hear their stories.*

One day, I took my grandsons to see their GreatGran. We stopped to say hi to Glen, who was also a resident when my dad was. Glen's dementia was quickly evident, but we found that conversations with Glen were entertaining, intuitive and eternally memorable:

Hi Glen! How are you today?

Watch out...the wagons are circling.

Oh...well...maybe they'll take care of me??

You can't depend on that. Did you pack for the coast?

Oh...are we going on a trip?

I can't remember, but pack anyway. I'm stopping at the morgue.

What are you planning to do there???

Drink. Would you like something?

Yes.

The boys listened respectfully with big eyes. As we walked away, 4-year-old Will said,

Nanie, can we go see the wagons?

Six-year-old Jackson said,

Will, there AREN'T any wagons!

The blend of reality and imagination was a beautiful snippet of fun for me.

The boys were excited to visit my dad because I had hinted of a possible present from GreatGran. In my wisdom, I had purchased Nerf blasters for both of them earlier. I carefully considered that they were quiet and I even got extra Nerf bullets so both boys would be happy.

Don't ever do this.

The word "blaster" should have been a clue. Both boys were so excited they immediately shrieked in glee and pointed them right at my bed-ridden father. I took them outside to run and shoot the plants, GreatGran watching through the window. His tears may have been the result of his stroke. Or maybe he was seeing himself as an innocent little boy.

When I took my precious granddaughter, Anna, I planned extra time. I just let her control the conversation and, at 16 months, she knew just how to communicate. Her vocabulary consists of 'Hi!' And 'Uh Oh', with creative vocal variety in between. She had entire conversations with residents. The sparkle in their eyes spoke back to her. Her laughter rang through the halls and won over every lonely heart.

Whenever I took Ernie Jr, our neurotic little dog, the residents looked at him, smiled and remembered their very first dog.

I will always hear my daughters, mothers themselves, walking in and gently saying, *Hi Granddaddy*! His smile of memory was loud indeed.

Attending a Sunday morning worship service brought a new meaning to "*when two or more are gathered in my name...* It was the hymns. Some of the old hands could not turn the pages, eyes could not read, minds seemed far away.

But it was the hymns. I could see the memories and belief in their eyes as they quietly followed the tunes and words that still sang to their hearts. Tears rolled down the cheeks of my stoic dad.

My husband is never in the pictures. He was always taking the picture, moving the furniture, or buying the milkshake, which was one of the few treats my father could eat. I remember the night my father had one of the caregivers help him dial our number and as he said hello, my husband began putting on his coat, knowing that I wouldn't be able to sleep unless we went to check on my dad.

There were the visits from my brother when he "took over the worry" so that I could…just live.

My cousin rode his motorcycle from San Francisco and stayed 10 days, having lunch with his uncle every day, listening to endless stories about my father's flying in Korea. His own father had been a pilot in WWII, but never returned home.

My dear sons-in-law watched endless football games in my dad's assisted living apartment, nearly suffocating from the 90 degree heat. They even made the trip to my dad's beloved Oregon State for a game in the fall of 2010.

The Village of love, professional support and tireless caretakers took care of my dad. For the last 5 years of my mother's life, my sons-in-law carried her inside their un-accessible homes so she could enjoy family dinners with us.

If I had known what it would take to care for my aging parents, I would have said I couldn't do it. But looking back…I appreciate what I learned and the value of my own inner strength. I treasure the Village. I could not have done this without them. In the end, it's not the smells of nursing homes, or the profound sadness of leaving a lonely parent in a nursing home knowing they'll never go home again. It's that when you really look at an old wrinkled hand next to a tiny new one, you feel the continuity of life.

And then you understand.

To everything there is a season and a time to every purpose under Heaven.

Tips for Nursing Homes

Dawna says

1. Some parents think they fear nursing homes when they really fear not being able to take care of themselves.

2. Care facilities have some wonderful caregivers and some people who are just drawing a paycheck, just like any other work environment.

3. Among the family we decided we were going to be frequent guests while mom was in the nursing home. We wanted the staff to see us coming and going at any hour. I guess the unspoken message was we wanted them to be vigilant about our mom's care.

4. I like all caregivers to think of me as pleasant but very aware and concerned about my loved one. I was probably more complimentary than most other daughters they ran across, but I also asked more questions than most others. It is the way I do my job when I have a loved

one needing care from others. For that, I don't make any apologies.

Marky says

1. I see skilled nursing facilities as necessary life-savers. And I was very glad they were available when my parents needed one.

2. For us, location was the determining factor. I worked full-time and I needed to be able to get there. I choose to be as close to my parents as possible when they needed me.

3. They are, by definition, institutions, and they exemplify much of what we dislike in nursing homes, the antiquated title. Sometimes, you just have to find the good.

4. Gather your village-and then let them help.

Chapter Ten

CAREGIVERS

BEING SURE OF ME

Marky writes

For the past six years, I have watched my parents leave. They enjoyed a wonderful retirement. Then the leaving began: their home, friends, activities, health, even their ability to reason and finally, they left me. My father is still alive, but the dementia has robbed him of…him. Though his personality peaks through, his eyes reveal loss. But he still knows me and I believe he is sure of me. I had no idea of the emotions that would engulf me, sometimes to the point of suffocation, as my mother's health began to deteriorate.

The first stroke left my mother using a walker. A few months after they moved to a retirement community in my state, Mom suffered another stroke, leaving her in a wheelchair, her personality much altered. Assisted living, a lift to move Mom from chair to bed and an accessible van created a new normal for my parents.

I could focus on the times I ran around putting out fires and organizing everything in sight and be awash with guilt. But this I know: Mom was sure of me and we did laugh. We had to. *The Van.* There were no van lessons. Whenever any of us-my brother, my husband, our daughters or their husbands would show up-my dad was so relieved to be "off duty" that he took off! It wasn't that he was unwilling or didn't love Mom. In fact, his love for her blinded him to many realities during the last five years of Mom's life. It was that being a caretaker is something that cannot be understood, unless one experiences it firsthand. Emotions catapult from fear, to grief, profound regret, anger and then to more guilt. As Mom's ability to assess situations lessened, my father's stress increased. But his constant mantra was

> *I left your mother with two small children while I fought in Korea. It's my turn to take care of her now.*

The first time I showed up to take her somewhere, my dad said *oh, it's easy* as he flew out the door to go somewhere with my husband. Mom was supposed to navigate up the ramp, position the electric chair and head straight forward to shotgun.

Okay, Mom, up you go....WAIT...STOP. I'm sorry-you're heading off the edge of the ramp.

I'll get it, honey. It usually takes me a few tries because your father makes me nervous, but I can do this.

Naturally, I felt terrible. I kept my mouth shut and Mom made it on the 3rd attempt. In she went and the lock clicked. Off we went. We were doing fine, until I drove (slowly, I promise) over a speed bump. NEVER go over one with an accessible van unless you're almost parallel to the bump and going one mile per hour. It sounded like the entire bottom of the van had been ripped off. Mom just laughed and said,

Oh-you should never go over bumps.

Amazingly, the van was still in one piece. Then we arrived at the doctor's office.

Okay Mom. Here we go.

Mom put the chair in reverse. Nothing Happened. This went on for about 10 minutes and I finally asked Mom if we were supposed to do anything.

Push the button, she said.

WHAT BUTTON? I quietly yelled.

I can't remember where it is.

Conversations with Mom were beautiful, funny and heartbreaking. Hysteria threatened as I dialed my cell phone. Mercifully, my dad answered and told me where the secret unlock button was. The van required a spot with space on the side for the ramp to open. That meant Mom had to navigate a sharp turn at the end of the ramp. More than once, I held my breath as she turned sharply, going right off the side of the ramp.

I also learned that if you're driving the van without a wheelchair in position, an ear-piercing alarm sounds-unless my dad had told you where that button was. At one point, the van needed some repairs and my son-in-law was picking it up. No one remembered to tell him about the alarm button. No one answered his calls of desperation. My daughter said he couldn't hear for two hours after he got home.

I will always remember the last day I saw Mom before we lost her to a stroke. I had taken her for a manicure (fashionable to the end) and as she was heading up the ramp, she went right off the edge. Fortunately, it was only a matter of about 6 inches and I was somehow able to navigate her back down the ramp for another try, my hands and heart shaking. Mom just laughed, her beautifully manicured nails flying joyously in the air.

Mom is gone now and recently, my dad had a stroke that required a move to an adult family home. His dementia creates many…interesting…conversations. Sometimes I just laugh and hold his hand and sometimes I promise I'll buy him the boat. But the hallucinations make my heart skip a beat. I took my two grandsons, ages 6 and 4, to see my dad with a promise to take them to see *Winnie the Pooh* at the "fee-ater", as little Will pronounced it. They love to see their GreatGran and even better-there was a beach to play on. The conversation started normally and then took a disastrous turn.

> *How are you guys today? Something terrible happened yesterday, my dad said.*

Ummm...what? I answered hesitantly.

There were a whole bunch of baby goslings walking across the yard and the lawnmower came along and chopped their heads off! answered my dad.

The boys' mouths dropped open! I quickly herded them outside, life jackets on, positioning myself to watch them play on the beach. As I changed the subject with my dad, his caregiver handed me some mail. Opening one, I stopped breathing as I realized it was a bill for $950 for a return trip on the ambulance after a recent emergency visit for my dad. Just as it dawned on me that this would not be covered, I looked out the window to see both boys happily playing in the water, up to their waists. I ran outside, reminding them that we couldn't go to the movie in wet clothes! Now I had two soaking wet, crying little boys:

We can't go to the fee-ater, Nanie???

Then, as I was hosing the layers of sand off, the caretaker said

I'm worried about your dad's blood pressure and the nurse hasn't called back yet.

I decided I needed *Winnie the Pooh*. We went to the store, bought new shorts, went to the movie and snuggled into the lovely world of Pooh.

Piglet sidled up to Pooh from behind.

Pooh! he whispered.

Yes, Piglet?

Nothing, said Piglet, taking Pooh's paw. I just wanted to be sure of you.

I do have regrets of missed moments with my parents, but I also know that the constant pulls of my life that defied those connections kept me sure of myself. And through it all, I know my parents were sure of me.

Handling Caregivers with Care

Dawna writes

I learned a great deal about working with caregivers while I was a working mom. As a full time career teacher with two daughters, quality caregivers were an important necessity. I learned the good ones were worth their weight in gold. Even if I were wealthy, I would never have been able to pay them an amount worth their value to us. Great caregivers are like great teachers, a profession I understand. They become caregivers because they choose to put someone else's needs before their own. They become wonderful at their job because they fall in love with someone you love and they are also completely trustworthy and competent. Parents and caregivers must share a general philosophy about raising children (or caring for seniors) and also possess a total sense of trust in one another. That trust is earned over and over again in a hundred little ways.

I once hired a young woman in her early twenties to care for my oldest daughter, Jodi, when she was just over a year old. She cared for my daughter for more than a year. Jodi became attached to her entire family. The caregiver's parents even became something akin to honorary grandparents to my daughter. In the beginning, I felt that Jodi was very well cared for. She was clean, fed on time, adored and was learning new skills each day. But when Jodi was about two and a half I began to see small signs that the gal was being less vigilant in her care for my daughter. I can't remember the details of what was gnawing at me. Maybe I noticed that she wasn't using enough diapers during the day, or that my daughter was writing on the wall or something else that gave me an instinct that she wasn't being well supervised.

This is before someone had invented a nanny cam, but my maternal instincts were sounding an alarm. I remember that I was at school worrying myself sick about this. I told my principal I was sick one day and had to go home. (I *was* sick with my concern about this situation). I arrived at home without notice in the early afternoon. The caregiver was on the phone on the first floor. Jodi was upstairs in the pajamas she had worn to bed the night before jumping up and down on her bed. I quite calmly fired the caregiver on the spot. Whatever my feelings on the inside, I always stay calm on the outside. (Remember the pressure I put on myself to calm my fighting parents).

This is before cell phones were prevalent. When she left I felt I had to make the dreaded call to her mother to tell her that I had fired her daughter and my reasons. I was distraught about it, but my trust had evaporated. I called my mom upset that night. Mom was a great listener in those days and a person I turned to many times for advice. She listened and commiserated. She agreed that I couldn't leave my daughter with someone I couldn't trust. She reminded me that I was a person with good judgment and that I should trust my instincts.

To help quell my guilt over the firing she said,

> *Why Dauna, you may have done this girl a wonderful favor. Sometimes we just have to learn a lesson the hard way.*

Then she went on to tell me a story about herself.

> *When I was young, I was hired for temporary help in an office. They gave me a long list of names and addresses to type on some envelopes for mailing. I could see that some of the addresses weren't complete. Maybe they were missing a house address or a city, I can't remember. I didn't want to seem stupid by asking questions, so I just typed up those addresses on the envelopes just as they appeared on the list and mailed them. I didn't think about the consequences. Day after day those envelopes just kept coming back to the office, being returned by the post office, one or two at a time. I began to dread the arrival of the mail. My bosses noticed the returned mail and fired me. I learned it was stupid not to ask questions. That experience did a lot to help me grow up and be more responsible in my next job.*

I'll never forget that story. Mom confirmed that my instincts and actions were sound and even relieved me of my guilt over firing someone. I had never fired anyone in my life and it made me quite uncomfortable. In an important way I had 'grown up' on that day. My mom had recovered from being fired. The girl and her family would also. The bottom line was I had to go with my gut and do what I thought was right for my daughter. Not too many years later I owned a business and had to learn to handle personnel issues frequently. That one experience had groomed me for this next important role.

Before long I was once again using that instinct with my younger daughter's hospital caregivers and then my mother's caregivers. I watched carefully and noticed everything that was happening. Almost always my daughter and mother knew who their best caregivers were. I knew when certain hospital nurses were assigned to my daughter's care overnight, I could sleep. When others were assigned it meant I would be up all night watching to make certain her needs were met. I was very liberal in my praise of the outstanding caregivers. *When someone goes the extra mile for your loved one and you notice and compliment that extra caring, the positive attention they share with your parent or child will increase exponentially.* But it was never a manipulation on my part. It was honest and sincere gratitude.

Later I heard cautionary stories from friends that recounted tales of caregivers who were exceptionally sweet to their elderly parents. But then once a strong relationship was established, those same caregivers began telling the seniors their own sad stories about their financial woes. I've heard more than one account concerning an elderly parent writing large checks to their caregivers because that caregiver shared a personal financial problem. One bank called an adult child I know to let them know their elderly father was writing large checks to a caregiver. This particular caregiver had convinced another senior from the same bank to also write her big checks. The bank noticed the pattern before the adult child was aware of it. These seniors happened to live in their own homes and depended on others for intermittent help, just like my mom.

One time I started to feel uneasy about one of Mom's cleaning women. My mom receives two hours of cleaning assistance each week through an agency for seniors who stay in their homes. This particular cleaning lady began doing some things for Mom that we children usually do. She took Mom out to lunch and once to get a haircut. We didn't know about these outings ahead of time. Mom told me that particular cleaning lady was going through a divorce and had money problems. She felt sorry for her. I admit my instincts were on alert. I talked it over with my daughter who is also close to Mom, and she agreed with my instincts.

Another time that same cleaning lady warned Mom not to tell her cleaning agency about some cleaning service she had done for Mom. That statement also made me feel uneasy.

We teachers tell children to be wary anytime someone tells them, "Don't tell anyone." I tried to begin a conversation with my mom about my fears on more than one occasion, but she was not at all open to my comments. So I let it go temporarily, but I stayed alert.

Before long the cleaning agency that employed the woman fired her. She was not allowed to have any contact with her former clients. I know this because the agency called Mother and told her so. Someone else might have had my same instincts. Months afterward I saw a card from the former cleaning woman on Mom's table asking mom to call her and listing her phone number. I asked Mom not to call her, but I'm not certain she complied with my wishes. Wasn't it Mom who once reassured me that my instincts were good? Yes, I could have called the agency and complained. But I was afraid my mom would find out and be furious with me. Mom felt genuinely cared for by this woman. These are not always easy situations to handle diplomatically. Sometimes solutions don't come neatly.

Through all of my decades of navigating through caregivers the wonderful, competent, professional caregivers far outweighed the ones I had to concern myself over. Kelsey had a caregiver who became so close to our daughter and our family that we named her Kelsey's Godmother even though she wasn't related to us by blood. Her name is Catherine and she enriched my daughter's life beyond what I could possibly describe in words.

In the hospital setting I learned to ask the nurses for their opinions and suggestions frequently. They took more time with patients and their families than the doctors did; and they also saw firsthand how a patient was reacting to a medication or treatment. Whenever my daughter or my mom were hospitalized, it was frequently a nurse who could suggest a slight change in the treatment that improved the patient's comfort and recovery. While doctors seemed focused on the recovery, nurses seemed more focused on the patient.

TIPS FOR CAREGIVER ISSUES

Dawna says

1. Ask people you know. Word of mouth recommendations are the best.

2. Both the parent and the adult child need to feel good about the caregivers. That is sometimes a challenge.

3. If a caregiver intimidates your parents *or* you, then they are the wrong caregiver for your situation.

4. Appreciate a great caregiver when you find one. Compliments go a long way.

5. Don't try to talk yourself out of a gut feeling. Have confidence in your judgment.

Marky says

1. I was lucky to discover that the caregivers truly loved both of my parents. But I found they saved their complaints for me. When I felt myself bristling against their need to vent, I realized that was part of my job.

2. My parents were in an assisted living facility, so the caregivers were already there. I found that most people in the field are there because they truly want to help elderly people.

3. Trust your instincts. Be observant. Ask questions.

4. Become friends with other adult children whose parents share the same caregivers. Compare thoughts and observations.

5. I know caregivers extended my parents' lives, and also the *quality* of their lives. For that I will always be grateful.

Chapter Eleven

CLOSE VS. FAR

I KNOW WHERE YOU LIVE

Dawna writes

Grandma is going to a holiday party in her own neighborhood tonight. Jodi took her to the grocery store today to pick up a food item for her to take. She just called me on the phone to ask when I could come to shampoo and style her hair. (Yes, it's my job, even though I'm not a stylist). When I get to her house she'll remember she doesn't know where her gift bags are (for the gift exchange) and ask me to find them. I better take a gift bag and tissue with me because it is easier to bring my own than finding them in Grandma's house. Maybe she forgot to even purchase the gift. I won't know this as I drive over there. She may want me to take her out to buy one after I do her hair. This is the minutia that fills our days on the good days when Grandma isn't sick.

Other days I take Mom to the clinic for a blood test or go to her house to pick up a specimen for a urinalysis. I then have to take it to the doctor and wait for the doctor's office to call with the results. If the test is positive I have to wait until the end of the doctor's day for him to call in a prescription. Why? *That's their procedure.* They don't care that I don't live in that community. After office hours I go to the pharmacy to pick it up, but they claim the doctor didn't call it in yet. I wait longer. Mom needs to get started on those pills. I keep asking the pharmacist but I can't call the doctor because his office will no longer answer the phone. After an hour and a half of waiting, there is nothing to do but drive home. The next day I start all over again and discover the doctor has sent it to the wrong pharmacy. This happens about one out of every six times. It seems to be a problem that can't be resolved even though I have described this scenario to everyone in the office, diplomatically I hope.

I sat in the teacher's cafeteria at lunch time and had co-teachers tell me how lucky I was to live close to my parents. Some days I wanted to protest, but then I hear their stories. They describe giving up vacations to travel out of town for their parent's operations and stay with them as they recover. My neighbor is an only child. Her father died a long time ago. Her mother lives about 1,000 miles away. She has given up every vacation for years to purchase a plane ticket and visit her mom, take her for critical doctor visits and hospital procedures. Her mom is losing her vision. She wants to move her mom closer, but knows it is going to be a sensitive topic to approach. I've talked to others who live much further away and haven't seen their parents in years.

Whether you live near or far from your aging parents, I know your address. We have an intersection here in my community where two streets cross. The names of those two roads which are unexpectedly joined at a corner are Grinn and Barrett. I suggest we all probably live at the intersection of Grin and Bear It in the community of Guiltsville, USA. It does seem that no matter how much I do, I still have to fight my own guilt. Why is that?

I'm trying to move just a little bit down the street from Grin and Bear It to Smile and Enjoy It. I know these moments are precious, made all the more so by the relentless movement of the hands on the clock. It seems the pages of my calendar flip over faster and faster now. No matter how challenging the responsibilities, I know that I will miss these days when they are gone. There is a country song that Trace Adkins sings that makes it hard for me to swallow and waters my eyes every time I hear it. Why? Anyone who hears it knows the words are some of the truest words ever put to music. He sings

> *You're gonna miss this*
>
> *You're gonna want this back*
>
> *You're gonna wish these days,*

Hadn't gone by so fast

These are some good times

So take a good look around

You may not know it now

But you're gonna miss this.

The words to that song perfectly describe this time in our lives. However demanding, I *do* know that I will miss these days later and want them back.

I'm back from doing Mom's shampoo now. We laughed hard together today. I've been sharing my writing with her. What a blessing that is for both of us. She loves hearing me read it to her. Today she told me a funny story about my dad and her that happened before I was even born. I had never heard the story before. If she were already gone, I would never have heard this story at all. Oh, it made us laugh so hard. There are lots of people who would give anything to have a great laugh with their mom. I try to stay aware of that blessing in the times that my patience feels stretched to the limit. I think I'll write about that story in this book. On my way home from Mom's house I laughed about it again and thought of a title for the story. I'm going to call it 'Eggs on the Floor'.

If you are lucky enough to have parents alive without a loss of their cognitive ability, do yourself a huge favor. Ask them to tell you a story they have never told you before. You will both treasure the experience.

CAREGIVING FROM AFAR. FROM NEXT DOOR. AND YOUR CLOSETS.

Marky writes

When my mother's health began to deteriorate, my parents were a 7 hour drive from my husband and me. Fortunately, they made the decision to leave their home and friends and move to a continuing care retirement community about 2 hours from us. The community was wonderful but quickly proved to be too far from us as Mom suffered another stroke that left her wheelchair-bound and needing more care. Because they had made the initial break from their long-time home, convincing them to move close to an assisted living facility close to us was easier. The actual discussion did not go well and ended with raised voices and tears.

But they did move.

I wouldn't describe the next 6 years of their lives as caregiving from afar, because they were only about 45 minutes away.

> *But any form of caregiving will rock the stability and emotional balance of an adult child's life.*

The telephone became my lifeline and my nemesis. It would ring. If the number was my parents' or their care facility, I would panic. Most calls weren't breath-taking emergencies, but enough were. I gradually became more immune to the phone ringing. At least I didn't hyperventilate or cross my fingers as much. At some point, the nurse from the facility became a good friend. On the plus side, the phone was my connection to doctors, therapists and daily chats with my parents.

I was a high school teacher, so my visits were limited to weekends. Since our married daughters lived fairly close to my parents, we settled into weekend visits that included an overnight with our children and grandchildren. Our grandchildren knew my parents as BabaGran and GreatGran and I know they will retain memories of my dad's flying stories and riding on BabaGran's lap in her electric wheelchair.

My sons-in-law were great sports fans and one even graduated from my parents' beloved alma mater, Oregon State, adding a permanent and cherished connection. I can still see my sons-in-law watching football in my dad's overheated apartment. Die-hard fans that they are, they never complained. I think they just brought more beer.

Our daughters visited when they could and we were able to include my parents in many family and holiday celebrations. I will always remember those dear sons-in-law carrying my mom into their inaccessible houses and then gently positioning her at the table or near the Christmas tree.

My husband's family parents and siblings literally spread from one side of the country to the other. His widowed mother settled near one daughter and the others did everything they could to support that daughter. I heard my husband call his mother often and as soon as he said "Hi Mom" there would be very long silences on his part, with one word interjections. His mother is…um…a talker. He and his siblings have done a remarkable job of rallying around the sister who lives close to their mother. The caretaking of my parents had taught us the importance of creating a united front, everyone stepping up to the plate and acquiring certain documents.

We talked with so many of our friends and sibling relationships were all over the board in terms of responsibility, getting along, as well as the ability and desire to help or not. All siblings or one sibling absolutely must talk with parents about their desires, expectations and plans for the future. The sooner this talk happens, the sooner everyone involved can assimilate expectations and absorb those into their own lives. Siblings also have to find a way to forgive siblings who aren't able or refuse to accept responsibility. In the end, everyone has to accept who they are. The talk absolutely must address housing desires, finances, end-of-life care and legal documents, including a Will, a Durable Power of Attorney and a Medical Directive.

The first conference call with my husband and his siblings included their parents. It was decided that later conference calls would just include the 4 children and spouses. Once they had the legal documents and a sense of what their parents wanted, it was easier to make other decisions. After their father died, the conference calls addressed issues concerning their mom and it was empowering for them to create a united front. A list was made about their mother's needs, then the list was divided into frontline and distance completion. While their mother's health and safety were always considered, they focused more on supporting the sibling living near their mother. This one focus went a long way in relieving everyone's stress and concerns, especially the resident sister.

During one hospital visit, the updates and phone calls were handled by my husband, the resident sister being the one to visit when she could. The first day in the hospital, his mother could barely talk. It became a waiting game for tests, diagnosis and prognosis. It seemed that his 92 year old mother was close to the end. But the phone call on the 2nd day sounded more like normal phone calls: silence from my husband. At one point, I heard my husband yell "MOM...you can't DO that!" After he hung up, he told me what his mother had said:

> *I LOVE the food here. I have never had such good broccoli. In fact, when my lease is up at my assisted living next month, I think I'll just stay in the hospital. I don't like the needles, but I sure like the food.*

I laughed so hard, I almost fell off of the couch. We live in a world of benefits, no benefits and out-of-control medical costs and fear of further escalation, but my husband's mother likes the broccoli. You can see why the conference calls did not include her.

I console myself with the thought that I did my best for my parents. My husband and his siblings can do the same. It's never perfect. It's just our best. And that should be enough to maintain our personal balance and sense of a job well done. Talk about a plan for your parents. Share it with all siblings, willing or not. Accept what you have to. Sit and just be with your parents whenever possible. And put your own house in order. That includes sharing the plan with your children, making difficult decisions so they don't have to. And clean out your closets.

TIPS FOR CLOSE VS. FAR

Dawna says

1. Accept whatever role you can play. If you can't be the one at the hospital during the day, be the one to care for the pet, or bring a meal to the caregiver in the hospital.

2. Far away? Send a fruit basket or snacks to the family members who are caring for your parent in the hospital.

3. Can you send money for a temporary home health aide?

4. Can you clean before your parent comes home?

5. Can you do laundry in your home for your parent while they are in the nursing home?

6. Are you better at deciphering medical bills than anyone else in the family?

7. Maybe you can call rehabilitation centers for information.

8. Allowing other siblings to do the bulk of the work of caregiving is simply not fair. But then, we know life isn't fair.

9. In the end, you will want to know you did your best. Try not to waste energy on siblings who don't see things that way. Use that energy for yourself and your own family. There is Karma, you know.

Marky says

1. Depending on your situations, distance can mean next door or across the country.

2. Living close might seem easier, but it's also a breeding ground for guilt, because you're not there every minute. Living far means guilt because time and logistics limit visits.

3. Finding caregivers in another city is easier because businesses are answering that need. If you can afford caregivers, you're ahead of many people.

4. If siblings are spread out, you can start with a conference call to get ideas and make plans.

5. In a perfect scenario, everyone will step up. Few *families are perfect*. Keep everyone in the loop and accept what each person will offer. Accept that it probably won't be "fair."

Chapter Twelve

OUR DADS

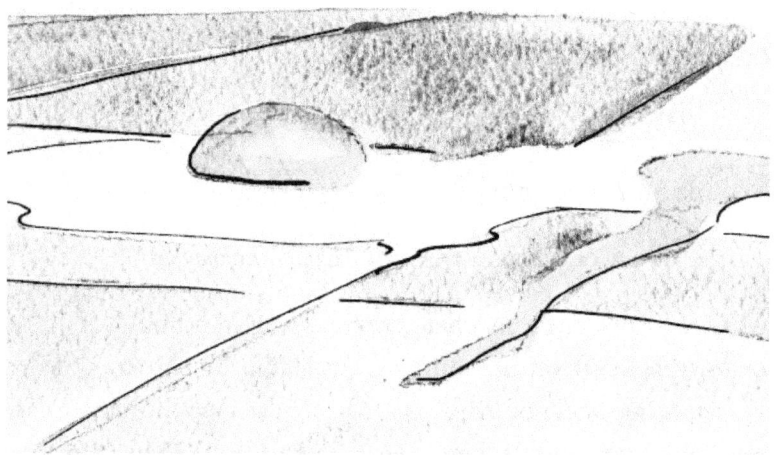

EGGS ON THE FLOOR
Dawna writes

My parents were eighteen years old when they were married. Their first apartment was only one room, not even a bedroom. Their bed was a murphy bed that pulled down from the wall. One morning in these very early days my dad asked for fried eggs for breakfast. Mom fixed them for him, but he complained about how they tasted and their consistency so mightily, that she finally had taken all his complaints she could handle. She picked up his dish full of fried eggs, turned it over and dumped those eggs right down on the floor. I don't know how the conversation proceeded from there, but Mom did tell me that neither one of them would clean those eggs up off the floor. For days they walked around those eggs. Remember this was a one room apartment not even big enough to fit a bed unless you were sleeping in it.

Mom only recently shared this story with me. We had a great laugh about it. But I couldn't help myself; I had to ask.

Mom, what ever happened to those eggs?

She continued her story.

They laid there for days until Mim came over for a visit.

Mim was my dad's mother…my future Grandma, but none of us were born yet. I thought to myself, 'Oh, she knew Mim was coming and got embarrassed to have her mother-in-law see those eggs and cleaned them up.' But no. When Mim saw the eggs she asked about them. Mom told her the story. Dad was there too and told his side of the story. But Mim was the one to clean up those eggs. My mom held her ground. So did my dad. This story, though funny today, so describes the scenario I was born into.

Mom was feisty. This story might make her seem a little crazed. But here is my honest opinion from someone who grew upside a house with my dad. Inside the home my dad was vain, critical, demanding and condescending. He was maddening enough to make June Cleaver throw eggs on the floor. Harriet Nelson, Donna Reed, or anybody else you want to name, the results would be the same…eggs on the floor. Mary Tyler Moore would have thrown those eggs on the floor and then shaken her fist in his face. Roseanne Barr would have pushed the refrigerator over on top of him and killed him dead.

Outside the home was another story. Outside the home Dad was vain (always vain), outgoing, charismatic, laughed easily and enjoyed being the life of the party. He didn't drink. He didn't need to drink. He ran around and caroused with women stone cold sober. He was larger than life in more ways than I can describe. He drove outrageously fast, dressed well, turned up the rock-and-roll music loudly and sang along. And always he had that outrageous, infectious laugh. He told jokes and laughed at them whether anyone else thought they were funny or not. He was his own best audience with that laugh.

Both of my parents were very attractive, but that is where their similarities ended. Dad had a "live for today" attitude. Have fun now. Don't concern yourself with tomorrow. Mom worried about paying the bills. Dad was frequently between jobs. Mother was reliable. Dad had circles of friends. Mom was supposed to work, come home, cook dinner and take care of the kids. And she did all of those things. Dad thought his having women on the side didn't hurt anybody. The reality was that it hurt everyone he really loved. I suppose lots of men have affairs, but I hope not. But my dad's womanizing was of epic proportions. We were all aware of his women and hurt by it.

But this book is supposed to be about elderly parents. Why haven't I told how hard it was to care for my father? He is eighty-eight as I write this and still driving for a living. He covers a three state area as a courier. He is agile. He will occasionally show up at an athletic function for a great-grandkid, walk a half mile or so from the parking lot to the stands and climb the bleachers which have no handrail without assistance.

Only a couple of years ago he did a headstand in my living room in front of his great-grandkids. I'm certain he could still do one today. In hospital buildings where he makes deliveries as a courier, he frequently climbs the stairs four or five stories. The truth is he doesn't like elevators. He once told me he waits to get on elevators until no one else is on them so he can hold onto the bar and do his deep knee bends as he rides between floors. I imagine the people who monitor the video films from the elevators get quite a kick out of him.

One time in my fifties I told my dad about someone my age who had just been diagnosed with cancer. His response?

I never even think about that kind of stuff.

He said this with such emphasis that I knew he was telling the absolute truth. There are other truths I don't know as facts, but I know *for sure* because I know my dad. He doesn't have life insurance or long term care insurance. He doesn't own a home. He has no savings. He lives day-to-day and never gives it a second thought. There will be no responsible conversations about money or plans for the future. I'm hoping one of his women will take care of him if he needs it. He once told me when he couldn't drive anymore he just wanted to be buried on that day, in a good looking car. He even described the car for me in detail, but I have to admit, I forget the description. Cars don't interest me much.

I'm grateful for his good health. I'm grateful someone else seems to care about him. I'm grateful that I am not angry with him. I got over that a long time ago. I hope my children and grandchildren are blessed with his longevity and agility. They deserve some good things from him. I felt like I needed to describe why he was largely absent from this book.

There's only one more thing I know for sure about my dad and his advancing age. If he does sometime end up in a nursing home, his caregiver will sooner or later throw his eggs on the floor. And I will understand.

A STORY TO TELL

Marky writes

The room of sixty 16 and 17 year olds was whisper quiet, all eyes focused on the elderly man as he slowly walked to the front of the room. It was a breath-holding moment for me because I was asking my father to share some of his most poignant memories with a room full of teenagers. I knew them and trusted their respect...but still. My father is a Korean War Veteran and like most high school juniors, springtime meant most were approaching the history around 1950. This was a combined history and English American Studies class with two teachers.

I had been a high school English teacher for about 15 years and had reached the point where teenage behavior, dress codes, and creative language were disguised and mitigated by the invisible energy that keeps all high school teachers coming back each day. The attitudes, excuses and lack of maturity are balanced and forgiven when the layers of self-protection evaporate...often revealing the realness and depth of their feelings. It had taken some time, but I had learned how to connect with them through humor, and some sort of sixth sense that told me when to tighten the reins. My parents had recently sold their home and were moving closer to my husband because of Mom's health issues.

This day, though, I had no idea what to expect-either from my father-or from my students. My own children were grown, with families of their own, so it had been many years since my dad had been around teenagers.

As my dad began telling his story, his voice was quiet, but their sharp ears didn't miss a word. I looked over at my teaching partner, the history "half" of our team, and she was lost in listening to someone who had lived this history she knew so well. My students knew something of the times from a letter my dad had written to my mom that I had shared with them. The date was July 22, 1944.

> *Dear Betty,*
>
> *If you aren't sure you love me, then don't read this letter. I love you and want to marry you. I'll be here until August 17th. We'll get B-26 training in 5 weeks instead of 10, then on to Shreveport, LA for 8 weeks overseas training and then overseas. The reason for this rush is that all the big shots in the European theater think the B-26 is the best ship to help the ground forces. They said the pilots were flying 3 missions a day and that is too much. With a wing span of 76 feet and being very heavy, it is difficult to land unless the pilot is well-trained. So darling, I'll make it easy. Will you marry me? You know why I want to marry you before I go overseas.*

They have a big area for feather-merchants to stay. (Officers were called ground-pounders.) When the war is over, we'll get a real home. My total pay will be $327 a month, which is $150 base pay, $75 flight pay and $102 rental allowance. I'll call you Tuesday night, because I'll have some money for the phone. Please answer real quick. I'll be waiting.

My students were very interested in flight training, unusual words and the idea of what one could live on in the 1940s, but when my dad walked in and begin to bring the letter alive with more stories, I witnessed the power of human connection. These computer-savvy, technology-influenced students were captivated by the age-old custom of storytelling. And these stories were true. My dad shared memories I had never heard. He was training on the B-26 Marauder in Del Rio, Texas when my mother arrived at the base. By the time he found her, she was hysterical because two planes had crashed as her bus drove in. She had no way of knowing if her fiancée was on one of those planes.

He told them of sleepless nights, 30 pounds of weight lost from an already slim body as he trained for hours in an airplane that had earned the nickname, *The Widowmaker*. He told them what it felt like to be in control of 76 feet of wings with only a co-pilot and a bombardier. He told them about losing his hearing from the deafening roar of the engines. He told them what it meant to trust someone with your life. He told them what it felt like when he learned a friend was gone. He told them what it felt like to visit the friend's grave many years later.

My father found his way to their young hearts.

Then came the questions. I didn't know which teenage personas I would hear that day but I have often thought that when presented with reality, sincerity and courage, teens respond with the same. Seventeen is a wonderful age, because naiveté is giving way to maturity. But the wonder is still there. Their eyes were riveted on the old Veteran and their need to know was palpable, in that state-of-the-art classroom in a school whose demographics told of successful, educated parents. They wanted to know how it really was.

The first question was

> *How did you feel when you dropped a bomb? Not how many bombs did you drop, but how did you feel?*

Silence. Then my dad said,

> *I was trained to do what I had to do. I felt and still believe I was fighting for the freedom you have today.*

The next question was

> *How do you feel about the war in Iraq?*

This was about 2 years into the war and I held my breath because these kids were sophisticated enough to understand what a political hotbed meant. Here is what he said:

> *I remember when my parents answered the door in 1944 to the uniformed officer with a telegram. The telegram started out 'we're sorry to inform you' and told of the loss of my older brother's plane in the Mediterranean Sea near Sicily. My mother was never the same. My nephew would never know his father. I would never want for you or your parents to*

> *receive such a telegram. I wish the world could find another way to solve problems.*

A Korean War Veteran. Sixty 16 and 17 year olds. Quite a contrast. But in that room on that day education happened. It had little to do with books, the state-of-the-art schoolhouse with many academic awards to its credit or even the teachers. It had to do with respect. When it's mutual, honest and real, we respond. My students felt entrusted and honored with my dad's stories and they recognized that it had taken an effort for him to be there. And they surely understood how he must have felt very far from his comfort zone. He had shared his stories and they had touched his experiences. There is no test that can assess such learning. There was one requirement and that was to write a thank you note. The old fashioned kind. And they did.

When asked what he thought about the day, my dad just said,

> *They listened. They really listened. You could have heard a pin drop.*

It's hard to imagine the courage it must have taken to fly the old airplanes, to leave a young pregnant wife, to leave your country. But think of this. If you do something that takes courage and you can tell the story 60 years later to 60 teenagers...and you can hear a pin drop as you tell your story...then I think you have a story to tell.

I've thought of this day many times. It was to become the beginning of 7 years of caregiving for my parents. The challenges were endless and often heartbreaking. But there are always trade-offs if you search for them. I was to learn who my father was.

Tips for Our Dads
Dawna and Marky say

1. Accept who your parents are. Even if they never truly accepted who you are, learn from that.

2. Work to let go of any anger. I choose to believe my parents did the best they could at parenting.

3. Embrace their history. Encourage them to tell you stories about their life that you may not have heard.

4. Look for ways to create memories together and connect the generations of your family.

5. Talking with moms (especially if you are a daughter) often comes easier. Find ways to get to know your fathers as well. When Mom's first stroke changed her so much I felt I lost her in many ways. But there was a benefit. My father and I had many talks that never would have happened.

6. When you do a project together sometimes the conversation flows more easily.

7. With my dad, I have to talk about cars, or at least listen as he talks about cars. It is just required.

8. Looking through old photos together prompts many memories and stories you may have never been told.

Chapter Thirteen
MEMORIES AND PATRIOTISM

DOCTORING AND THE VA

Marky writes

Since I live close enough to my parents, the past 7 years have included more doctor and hospital visits than I can actually remember. Some of the memories are easy to block out because you hear the kind of information that underlines the futility of the innumerable band-aids of aging. But you continue to take them because just as when Casey walked up to bat, *hope springs eternal within the human breast.* My father is a veteran of WWII and the Korean War, so he is eligible for care at a

Veteran's Hospital, which those who are familiar will know as the VA.

I have a few memories of my father returning from the Korean War. My mother took care of my brother and me in a small house in Lubbock, TX. One memory is that our next door neighbors had an outhouse. Now you know a bit about the neighborhood. I also clearly remember the day my father received the Distinguished Flying Cross. He stood out on the field with another pilot and the wife of a pilot who did not return. I remember asking my mother why there was a lady out there and I will never forget her answer:

> *That lady's children no longer have their daddy. He isn't coming home.*

Even my four-year-old mine understood.

Since my father did not talk about his flying days, his military history was not a central part of my life until the days of taking him to the VA. My parents lived about 30 miles north of me and the VA was 25 miles south. So the trip was an all-day affair and if my husband wasn't available, I took the day off from teaching.

My parents were of the generation who did not question the doctor. They were not what we like to call "proactive". That meant that if the appointment was set for Tuesday at 8:00 am, my dad would just say ok. This is how our conversations would go:

> *Have you heard from the VA about your (audiology, urology, heart) appointment?*

Oh yeah. They called two weeks ago.

Ummm-what did they say?

It's this Tuesday at 8:00 am.

Daddy!!! I work-remember? I can't get a sub that quickly!

Oh.

What is the appointment for?

Something about my heart.

What is the number I can call to change the appointment?

Well, let's see. It's here somewhere...

After endless-I really mean endless-phone calls, I created a catalogue of possible connections with the VA. Nothing was ever really for sure but I got better at figuring the system out. I will say that the care my dad received from the VA was excellent. But the communication system was the cause of so much frustration for me. But maybe it was me. I was trying to connect my organized-privileged-pro-active life to a system that was created in another era. That system is not equipped to handle the influx of needs of the military of today. This is what I will always remember:

Long rides where I could talk with my dad.

A maze-like building with additions marking our eras of war.

Lonely men. And so many of them appeared to be without means.

A dated building full of dedicated medical personnel caring for those who have served our country.

My dad retired in the years when companies also offered medical benefits, a concept which is completely foreign to us now. I often tried to get him to move his care to the private sector using the argument that others needed the VA more than he did. He did relent some, but always unwillingly. I never understood why. Until…

When my husband and I visited friends in Washington, DC, we toured as many of the memorials as we could. The Korean War Memorial took my breath away. Maybe it was the life-sized GIs, forever cast in bronze poses. Maybe it was the indelible memory of my dad receiving his medal. No-here is what it was: as we moved to the front to take pictures, there was a group of young Koreans, clearly born long after the Korean War. The joy in their faces told me a story. I saw what it meant to them to finally reach the memorial to those who had given them freedom. It is not a forgotten war. My dad was part of making their joy possible.

I wish I could still take him to the VA.

Making Memories
Dawna writes

Maybe it is because I felt so grown up even when I was a child. Does that make me an old soul? Maybe it is because I taught school for so long and I was used to creating classroom experiences, and memorable programs and gifts for parents. I don't know exactly why, but I understand the importance of making memories. I go out of my way to plan experiences that I believe my grandchildren will remember long after I'm gone. I include their great-grandparents whenever I can.

Some of those experiences work fabulously, like a well-directed movie. Sometimes those activities flop. More than once I've heard a grandchild ask with a whine,

Why are we doing this?

My reply is always the same.

We are making a memory.

Sure I'd rather the memory be one of those warm and fuzzy moments, but even bad memories have a way of making you laugh or form a camaraderie of complaint later in life. The wheels in my head are always turning.

What can we do, that we haven't already done, to create a memory?

Sometimes I'll even plant a seed for a memory. When you sit outside on the screened in porch at my house, you can hear train whistles blow as they pass a certain intersection. When grandkids are small they always seem to notice train whistles. "Ah!…choo-choo train," they'll say whenever the whistle blows. This happens frequently in the summer months at my house. I told them a story about my own grandparents who lived near a church. At their house when I was a little girl, I heard church bells ring marking every hour. Ringing church bells still remind me of being at my grandparents' house.

You will always remember being at your grandparents' house when you hear a train whistle.

I actually tell them that, like it's a homework assignment or something. I have no shame when it comes to making a memory.

But in 1990 one special memory came our way that I didn't have to plan. My daughter Kelsey had been battling cancer for two years at the time. I was the president of the support group for parents of children with cancer at Children's Hospital in Cincinnati. The support group sent me to Washington D.C. to the national Candlelighters conference. Candlelighters was a respected international organization of parents of children with cancer. Parents and their children were invited. My husband couldn't go but I went and took my mom and my daughter. Kelsey was seven at the time, I was in my early forties and my mom was in her mid-sixties. Three generations of us were all visiting our nation's capital for the first time. It was such a moving experience for which I will always be grateful.

Small scenes still come to mind twenty some years later. Hearing a speaker from St. Jude's telling the parents in the audience that children were surviving in direct proportion to the courage of their parents as they were trying new procedures and protocols all the time. Going to the top of the Washington Monument and looking at all the scenes of the city. Standing in silence at the Viet Nam Memorial engraved with the names of so many of my baby boomer contemporaries. Listening to a military band play patriotic songs beneath the Washington Monument. Seeing the Lincoln Memorial for the first time. Touring the White House…all these places we had only seen in pictures or on television in our past. Mom talking to the guard standing at the driveway entrance to the White House. Observing from a distance a celebration of a Bill being signed on the White House lawn. It turns out it was the Americans with Disabilities Act which would feature so prominently in Kelsey's future as her intelligence was forever altered by the effects of brain radiation at such a young age. What are the chances that we would be there at exactly the time they were signing that particular Bill? It was an intersection of coincidences.

But the most moving of all the memories, the mental picture that will be forever in my mind is standing around the big evergreen, the national Christmas tree, the permanent one that is decorated each year for the holidays. It was dusk as we looked at the back of the White House. We held candles as we created much too large a circle around that tree, parents, children cancer patients and some extended family members. We stood there in silence as we held those candles and dusk faded to darkness. Finally someone started singing.

We are the world,

We are the children...

All joined in. I'll never forget the goose bumps on my arms. Kelsey almost bald, my mom, and me; three generations of hope. I'm glad we were there together. It won't be much longer until I will be the only link in that chain left on this earth. But I will treasure that memory and hold it close to my heart for the three of us.

Chapter Fourteen

ACCEPTANCE

RED LEATHER MARY JANES, A LADDER AND BENNY GOODMAN

Marky writes

As I looked at Anna's red shoes, I saw my mother. Anna wears little tiny size 3 red leather Mary Janes. The toes are scuffed, because she crawls everywhere and those scuffs are completely endearing to me. My mother spent the last 5 years of her life in a wheelchair. At times, it seemed all I could do was put out fires…the fires involved with life in a wheelchair. The challenges were endless. But this isn't about challenges. This is about the small beauties of life: the ones that stop your breath, the ones that bring the quick tear, the ones that release the power of a memory that ambushes you with surprise.

My mother had always loved cute shoes and she loved to dance. But she was a child of the Depression and cute shoes weren't easy to come by. Plus, she had very narrow feet. In later years, after the children were raised, she could finally afford shoes and she bought expensive ones, because they catered to narrow feet. Very classy actually, but not faddish or cute.

A wheelchair does offer one advantage. You can wear any shoes you want, no matter how narrow your feet are. I bought Mom a pair of red leather Mary Janes. By this time, my parents were living in an assisted living center because of Mom's medical and assistance needs. Nice people, but not very many cute shoes. Mom's red leather Mary Janes were cute, though, and people noticed. She loved them. I can still see those red shoes, poised there next to each other on the footrest of the wheelchair, just waiting to go dancing. I smiled every time I looked at them.

Mom died before Anna, her 3rd great-grandchild, was born. But she knew that her youngest granddaughter was pregnant with a little girl, giving Mom great comfort. Baba, as her first grandchild had named her, had worried that she would die before Ashley got pregnant. It so happened that I gave Ashley the little red leather Mary Janes at a baby shower a week before Mom died. Since they were a size 3, they were put away until Anna was a year old. Then one day Anna and I were playing on the floor and I attempted to pose her for a picture. Of course, you don't pose a baby for longer than 2 seconds, but those 2 seconds took my breath away: Anna's shoes. My daughter had dressed her in the little red shoes for the first time that day. As Anna danced out of her pose, I saw my mother's red shoes. They weren't lined up like red soldiers at attention, on a wheelchair. They were…dancing. I know this about Anna: she will love shoes. And she will dance, just like her BabaGran.

Grandchildren do indeed keep the circle going, but seeing the world through their eyes opens your eyes and heart in ways you never felt before. Anna's two older cousins thought BabaGran was "hot stuff" because they could ride on her lap on her wheelchair, or we would push them through the halls of the assisted living facility on Mom's walker.

When my mother died, Will was almost three years old. He had loved BabaGran and as he processed where she must have gone, he quietly shared his insight with me. He told me that he could fly up to heaven to see BabaGran whenever he wanted and that he might be able to get a ladder for me to come too. I think some grandparents have a gene that allows them to settle with confidence into whatever age a beloved grandchild is. I quickly made an appointment with Will to go up that ladder. But there are rules associated with this grandparent gene and one is that you don't ask logical questions, *like why can't I just fly with you?*

If I asked Will if he had found the ladder, he demurred. I was…disappointed. While part of me wondered if I was losing touch with reality, my grandparent gene was picturing myself as Vector in *Despicable Me*. But he would bring it up occasionally and promised me that he was still checking for the ladder. He hadn't figured out how the ladder part would work, so he wouldn't commit. One day, at his older brother's soccer game, thunder loudly intervened. Will asked his mom

> *Is that BabaGran talking from heaven?*

The thinking of an almost-three-year-old is logical, creative and a match for Pixar and their like any day!

During this ladder-processing time, I was also helping my dad cope with his grief and loss. When he expressed his loneliness, I told him that I often talked with Mom and that he might consider doing that. He wasn't impressed. Then one day, my dad called to say he was dancing with my mom. My response surprised him. Without missing a beat, I said,

> *Don't step on her red leather dancing shoes.*

My dad was quiet, but I could hear Benny Goodman in the background.

From Anger to Gratitude

Dawna writes

I was teaching high school when my husband just appeared at the school door. I knew in that moment, but I didn't want to hear the words. We stepped into a small office and he said them anyway,

> *Kelsey's cancer has come back.*

The hospital could reach his cell phone easier than contact a teacher in a classroom. I think it was the one time in our eleven year battle with Kelsey's cancer that I let my husband see me fall apart. When two parents are both worried over a child, each goes out of their way not to distress the other one.

I don't know the pain of saying a final good-by to a parent. I won't try and pretend that I do. My parents are both still alive. I do know that when my mother is gone I will miss her for the rest of my life. I'll probably miss even those embarrassing moments when her raucous humor makes my face turn bright red in front of others.

But I have survived what I believe may be an even more challenging farewell. I had to come to a place of acceptance over losing my sixteen-year-old daughter to brain cancer. I can only believe that walking that path that no parent wants to ever imagine, will at least be helpful to me when it comes time to say good-by to my parents. I wish I hadn't had to learn things that I already know.

Here are some things I've learned for certain. To be honest, these are facts we all know in our guts, but knowing them in kind of a subconscious way and actually *living* them are two very different experiences. At least that is what I discovered.

> It doesn't matter how much you love, want, need or care about someone, we are, *all of us*, only temporarily on this earth. Of course, you know that. The teenagers would say… "*well, duh*". But do you really *know* that? It's nothing to worry about. Worrying doesn't help or change anything. It is just a fact. *But we need to <u>live</u> like we really understand that concept.*
>
> All we can truly control are the days we spend with each other while we still have one another. The sooner we come

to realize that, the fewer regrets we will have when that time is over.

All we can do is all we can do. I drove myself close to crazy reading everything, learning everything I could, watching every procedure, weighing every decision on treatment options, and ultimately the final outcome is the same. My daughter is gone. That was probably my hardest lesson to learn. I was willing to do anything to save her life. But nothing could save her life. All we can do, really *is* all we can do.

I only ended up with a couple of regrets. But even a single regret will drive you nuts. If I were required to make a list of everything we did right, I could list dozens of things. But when someone dies it is hard to focus on those at first. We first just dwell on the regrets. We have to forgive ourselves before we can remember all the right things we did.

Life will occasionally continue to put hurdles and challenges in front of you even after you have faced the ultimate pain… the loss of a loved one. When you are low, those regrets will seep back in. It takes effort to push them back down. But it is possible and worth the effort.

Anger is a natural part of the grieving process. You can be mad. I was furious. I remember beating on my steering wheel and screaming at God while I was driving one day. Is it even smart to scream at God? Probably not. But God had to watch His child die and I believe He understands my anger.

<u>But if you stay mad, it ultimately only poisons you.</u> It also robs the people around you. It does nothing to honor the person you loved and lost. *Anger does not prove how much you loved them.* You honor a loved one by being grateful for the time you had with them.

You also honor a loved one by sharing memories of them… keeping their story alive. Only one of my grandkids is old enough to have known Kelsey, but *all* of them *know* her through the stories they've been told. They frequently ask me to repeat those stories. One of them was born only a week after Kelsey died. Kelsey is that grandchild's middle name.

There was one thing that really helped a great deal. I read an article within the year before Kelsey died. I wish I knew the magazine, author or title. I'm embarrassed I don't. I really owe this author such gratitude. Kelsey had already battled cancer, but had been cancer free for ten years at the time I read the article. At that point I was hopeful the cancer would never return.

In the article an adult woman was describing her brother. He was the star of the family. He was athletic, the president of his high school class, outgoing, charming, and successful in every way. The author was his younger sister. She kind of lived in his shadow but also adored him like everyone else. Her larger than life brother went across the country to college. He had a fluke accident, fell in the shower, hit his head and died quickly. His younger sister (the author) was at home with her parents when that awful phone call came in. She watched her parents receive this horrible news over the phone. She wrote

> *"I knew in that moment, that I had not only lost my only sibling, a brother I had adored, but I had lost my parents as well. It was true. They never recovered from it. In essence I lost them as parents on the same day my brother died."* (The quotation marks are mine. I can't remember her exact wording, but the story struck me so much that I know I have paraphrased the essence of that conversation.)

Those words hit me and ricocheted through my body like a lightning bolt. *I promised myself that very second that I would never allow that to happen.* If the worst happened and the cancer returned and we lost Kelsey, I would never allow my other daughter to lose her mom too.

Jodi, my only other child, lost her only sibling when Kelsey died. She would NOT lose her mother as well. That would be a double whammy she didn't deserve. Nor would my grandkids lose their Grammy.

Additionally, my students would <u>not</u> have less of a teacher. They would have a wiser teacher. It was a choice I made in an instant. Living that choice took plenty of courage, but I'm proud to say that I *did* it and continue to live that choice. There were some tough times. Kelsey died at the end of her sophomore year. I taught seniors and I dreaded the year that would have been her senior year in high school. It was made worse by junk mail. At our home she received every invitation for senior pictures, every college solicitation, every graduation gown sales gimmick or advertisement for class rings that a living child would have received. Outrageous, unnecessary attacks came from the mailbox each day. But I learned to mentally "delete" those items just like any other unwanted intrusion.

First when we are young our parents teach us how to live. Then when we become parents a turnabout occurs. Our children teach *us* how to live. We learn to model positive behaviors *for* them. They are more spontaneous, experience wonder in small things, are accepting and forgiving in ways that we adults have sometimes forgotten. We watch them and learn to become better people.

Kelsey taught me so many things. She taught me how to face a disease and refuse to let it overwhelm you. She figured out her own philosophy when she was only five. We were never allowed to speak about her cancer in front of her. That was *her* rule. She also never, never spoke about cancer to us. I know it sounds like I'm making this up or overstating it, but I swear that it is true. It was Kelsey's way of not letting cancer run her life. She was never a little girl with cancer (except to people in the community who discussed her in that way). She was Kelsey, a little girl. Some years her cancer care demanded huge amounts of her days, but she refused to give it one second of conversation. Was this denial? I don't think so. I think it was her way of letting the disease know that *it* didn't control *her*.

I can tell you honestly that her standard didn't come from me. I needed to talk about Kelsey's cancer and I did, but never in front of her because she wouldn't allow it. Sometimes I embarrass myself when I realize how many people I tell if I have a sinus infection. I am in awe of her wisdom and self-control in not allowing a disease to run her life. How could one so young be so wise?

But, if I'm honest, I think there was even another motivation at work within her. Kelsey was an extraordinarily empathetic kid. Even at age five she did what she could to protect us, her parents. It sounds like an absurdity, but you had to know my daughter to know the truth of it. We struggled courageously to hide our fears and worry over her health from her, but she saw it in our eyes and did all she could to protect us. She consistently did that right up to the end at age sixteen. She struggled too long to stay alive for us. Her dad finally had to give her permission to die. He had to reassure her we would be alright. She had such a calm acceptance of her situation that my child taught me how to die with grace, courage, and caring. This is a lesson a mom should never have to learn from her child.

After the grief what is left? I'm glad to report there is plenty of gratitude left for her life. Kelsey left her earthly home in 1999. There is finally a lot of laughter over the times we had, the funny things she said and did. I am especially grateful for the lessons she taught me. Maybe it is the teacher in me, but Kelsey's whole life seemed to be a giant lesson for me. The ending wasn't a lesson I wanted to experience but it eventually taught me a great deal in spite of the anguish. She made me a much better person, teacher, parent, and friend.

Let me share one of Kelsey's lessons with you. Beginning when Kelsey was a preteen, every once in a while she'd make a request.

Mom, can we have a robe day?

This usually happened early on a weekend morning while we were still in our robes and I was thinking about all I had to accomplish that day. During all the years my two daughters were growing up, I was a busy teacher. My weekends were filled with laundry, athletic events, grocery shopping, grading papers, and errands I couldn't accomplish during the week. My weekdays were largely focused on meeting the needs of other people's children or helping Kelsey with her homework.

I came to understand what 'robe day' meant for Kelsey. Robe day meant that we weren't going to be rushing anywhere. Who runs errands in their robe? Robe day meant we were going to stay home…together…all day …in our robes.

The first challenge of robe day meant that I had to shut off the mental 'to-do' list **screaming** in my head.

On robe day we would crank the music up loudly. We would clean and dance together. We'd bake cookies or brownies. We'd simply hang out around the house. We'd pop popcorn and watch her favorite movie, *Pretty in Pink* one more time, together.

Robe day actually meant,

I need you mom. I need you all to myself.

One really good robe day could fuel us both for a month or two. The older I become the more I cherish the memory of those days together in our robes. I wonder why I didn't have the wisdom to ask for them. I'm so grateful that my daughter did.

It occurs to me that my mom now spends lots of days in her robe. Maybe I just need to take my robe to Mom's house and spend a day in it. I need to look through old snapshots with her for this book. We can laugh together about old times or wish we still were our former weights. It sounds like a good plan. Where's my robe?

Tips for Acceptance

Dawna says

1. Grief has a different path and time table for each person. Allow yourself the time you need to grieve.

2. Being angry is part of the grieving process. But staying angry only hurts you.

3. Try to understand, that all you can do, really *is* all you can do. Try not to drive yourself crazy second guessing your decisions.

4. Everyone loses their parents sooner or later. It's part of a natural process. No parent would want to see their child suffer tremendously over this loss.

5. Honor your loved one by keeping their memory alive with stories.

6. After your parents are gone ask yourself, "What would my parents want to see happen in my life?" Focus on living well. That is a wonderful way to honor them.

Marky says

1. When my beloved younger brother died early in the process of caring for my parents, I couldn't imagine coping without him. It was to prove even harder than I thought but I did cope.

2. Losing my brother first probably made me better able to accept the loss of both of my parents. I would say my grief was somehow *gentler* with my parents. They visit

my heart often. I feel and hear them in many places. Time does heal.

3. I admit to a sense of relief every time the phone rings. The worry had become a constant default in my life.

Epilogue

HOME BEFORE DARK

Marky Olson

My father died the night before my husband and I were to leave on a long-awaited trip to Hawaii. The trip had been planned for a year to celebrate my husband's milestone birthday and we were taking our kids and grandkids. The trip was appropriately paid for with money my dad had given me when he sold his beloved fishing boat. The week before we left, it was clear to all of us that the end was near. We had called in Hospice and I spent those last few days with my dad, making my peace with saying good-bye when he was still alive. At least that's what I told myself. The phone rang just after we had gotten in bed the night before the early departure.

The nurse told me my dad was gone.

I know my father did that for me. Many would say it was coincidence or wonder how I could consider leaving before he was gone. But the past 7 years of caring for my parents has granted me a level of maturity and wisdom we all want. I have learned to do what I can, be there when it counts and deny the ever-lurking power of guilt.

My parents' journey included a continuing care retirement community, as assisted living facility, several stays in skilled nursing facilities and finally, an adult family home. They were not able to stay in their home in central Oregon, near their friends because of Mom's health. They made the first decision to move closer to my husband and me, which made the rest of the moves far easier. They spent 6 years at the assisted living facility and it became a home for them with friends and activities. Mom's need for extensive care was answered and the caregivers became friends. I will always cherish my friendship with the nurse from that facility. When my mother died, we had a memorial right there, all of the residents appreciating the warmth and beauty my mother brought to the world. My father was to live there another year, benefitting from the established friendships and caregivers, whose care for him went far beyond the job description.

I miss my dad. But I came to realize that I couldn't take Mom's place and it was time for him to be with her again. Watching a parent die slowly means accepting each robbery of independence until finally, the joy of having them is outweighed by diminished existence. That's life. That's the way of it. Denying acceptance creates roadblocks that govern much of our lives. But denial does buffer acceptance, cushioning its permanence. And finally, acceptance is freeing. I will grant it that.

Conversations with my dad became heartbreaking or entertaining, depending on whether I was in an acceptance or denial state on a given day. About 4 months before my dad died, we returned late from a trip and stopped to visit him. He was already in bed, but still awake. The conversation went something like this:

When are you going to be home?

I'm home Daddy!

Okay…so you'll be here in about two hours?

I'm here NOW!

I got all of the tomatoes picked up, but did you get the ball hoop last night?

The last question was directed at my husband and we just looked at each other as fragments of his memories revealed themselves to us like escaping butterflies. The mystery was to be solved when I called one of his life-long friends 4 months later. I called King, a grade-school friend from Portland, Oregon to tell him that my dad had died. He began telling me stories about their antics in the 1920s and 30s. King told me they used old barrel hoops and staves to fashion a basketball hoop, which they attached to my grandparents' garage. I was reminded that, as a child, I thought it wondrously cool that Grandpa's garage faced the alley. They shot basketballs in those hoops for hours on end. I asked King if he had any thoughts on tomatoes. He said,

Yes, your grandmother had tomatoes growing on the side of the garage and we had to pick all of those tomatoes before we could play basketball.

The mystery conversation was solved, leaving me with a lifetime memory of my father and his friend as young boys. What a gift.

My father was known for his beautiful snow-white curls. Even his final caregiver at the adult family home took great pleasure in taking care of my dad's hair. I think that is what I loved best about her. When my dad died before the trip, I was somewhat comforted with the fact that all decisions had been made, papers signed and confirming phone calls completed. My parents had chosen cremation and since Mom had died two years previously, this was not new territory for me. I went on the trip with a mixture of relief, grief and a sense of peace. Just after we returned, I began processing details and thoughts. I suddenly realized I didn't have a lock of my dad's hair.

Panic and regret set in.

My youngest grandson is 4 years old and doesn't appreciate his curly hair…and I hadn't thought to get a lock of my dad's hair to someday share with this grandson who is very close to my heart. I called the funeral home to take care of payment and some details, lamenting my oversight. The response brought one of those moments of "rebirth" that we experience a few times in life. Had I not gone on the trip, I would have attended to the bill promptly. The funeral home does not complete arrangements until the bill is paid. I now have a cherished lock of my dad's hair. When Will is old enough and the time is right, I will share the curls of his great-grandfather and the history that is his.

I lived in New York State when I was old enough to drive. You could drive only during daylight at 16, but not after dark. I think the only time my father ever really got mad at me was when I got home one night after dark. My relationship with my father was the best. It was a treasure and in the final years when my mother struggled mentally, I became closer to my dad. Then, the year after Mom died, we spent time together and I really learned who my father was. Unconditional love is what all of us want.

But we also have to be home before dark.

Home Before Dark

I knew my parents would age…someday.
Emily Dickinson told me
Because I could not stop for death/
he kindly stopped for me…
But living it laughs at knowing it.
Overturning the hourglass of sand means feeling
each grain as it falls.
e e cummings said *i carry you in my heart*
Letting go of a parent one grain at a time is like living life in
reverse is what I say.
Profound strength helped me carry them…
Seven years of letting the grains go from my heart.
I did put out most of the fires,
which kept me from sitting and holding my mother's hand.
But I forgive me.
Had I done so, Mom and I, we would have cried too much.
From his nursing home bed, my father's wandering mind said
Home before dark.
My mind wondered: *am I 12 years old again, or will he be with*
Mom tonight?
A forest of fear. But pocket parks of love everywhere:
A doctor who held my father's hands as he
said *we must let my love of 65 years go.*

The tears of young caregivers who cherished the wise haven of
old age.
My husband, always my home.
My daughters, walking slowly into the hospice room.
Sons-in-law watching my dad's beloved OSU
Beavers in his 90 degree apartment
…carrying Mom into their un-accessible
homes for family dinners.
A beloved 3 year old grandson who explained to me about
ladders to heaven.
Sit beside the ocean and say goodbye-
you'll see. The circle of life shines all the way to heaven.

Recommended Reading

Get a Life ~ You don't need a Million to retire well, By Ralph Warner

How to Say it to Seniors ~ Closing the Communication Gap with Our Elders, By David Solie, M.S., P.A.

The Longevity Project ~ Surprising Discoveries for Health and Long Life from the Landmark Eight-Decade Study, By Howard S. Friedman, Ph.D. and Leslie R. Martin, Ph.D.

Cicero ~ On a Life Well Spent, Preface by Benjamin Franklin, Levenger Press

READ BLOG POSTS BY DAUNA EASLEY AND MARKY OLSON

www.CaregivingElderlyParents.com

www.icareinsite.com (Marky Olson)

www.DaunaEasley.com (Dauna Easley)

Informational Websites and Contacts

www.eldercare.gov – Search by zip code to connect with your area agency on aging. This valuable resource will also connect you with the Long-Term Care Ombudsman in your area.

www.SeniorHelpers.com - The Senior Gems Your Guide to Supporting Family Members with Dementia DVD

www.icareinsite.com – Obtain current, translated medical records for your loved one.

www.livingwellmagazine.com – excellent articles and information

www.sageminder.com – contacts and information

www.maturitymatters.com – ideas for better health

www.AgingDeliberately.com - excellent source of information

Special Mention

www.gcmathews.com, Illustrator for *Caregiving for Your Elderly Parents*

www.howardhowell.com, Technical support

www.patricksnow.com, Publishing and marketing support

www.fusioncw.com, Design, format and layout

www.ingramcontent.com/pod-product-compliance
Lightning Source LLC
LaVergne TN
LVHW020928090426
835512LV00020B/3267